Wilderness and marshes, the vast wild Northland . . . forest thick and dark, pathless and soundless, the pines and aromatic cedars, the silvery fogs, well-trodden Indian trails, the white birch, and the tall spruce-spires, the bald Northern cliffs bathed in sunshine . . ."
—*Constance Woolson 1870*

To my friend Rose Marie
Thank you,
Elizabeth Lenco-Downs

LENCI STUDIOS

Lizzy

Love, Laughter, and Tears . . .

A SPECIAL COLLECTION
*Of Stories And Poems
From . . .
A Minnesota Daughter*

Elizabeth Lenci–Downs

LIZZY - US Copyright 2012 / 2015 - Elizabeth Lenci–Downs.
LIZZY - US Copyright 2017 - Elizabeth Lenci–Downs.
A Spoonful Of Sugar - US Copyright 2017 - Elizabeth Lenci–Downs.

Photography: The John Noyes Downs Collection - Sudan, Minnesota.

LIZZY - Love, Laughter, and Tears
First Printing - 2017.

LENCI STUDIOS
ISBN: 09711905-3-4

Grateful acknowledgement is made to John Noyes Downs for a special selection of photographs used in this book; The author appreciates permission to reprint Etching: The Brig - by ship artist Gordon Grant, in *The Book of Old Ships - From Egyptian Galleys to Clipper Ships,* by author Henry B. Culver, 1942. Reprinted: Dover Pictorial Archive Series ©1994. With Permission, Dover Publications, NY.

All rights Reserved

All rights reserved under International and Pan-American copyright conventions. No part may be used or reproduced in any manner whatsoever without prior written permission of the author or Lenci Studios with the exception of brief quotations embodied in critical articles and reviews. Discount is available for groups and retailers.

For information or to order contact:

THE SOLE PUBLISHER OF THIS BOOK
LENCI STUDIOS
P.O. Box 19206.
Fountain Hills, AZ. 85269.
480–816-3875
www.LenciStudios.com
Official website – PayPal – Amazon.

By ELIZABETH LENCI–DOWNS

NONFICTION

I Heard My People Cry:
One Family's Escape From Russia
1978-1950 true story of Germans from Russia - the Huebert families, and told to the author by survivor Louise Huebert, Gerick.

Six Girls On A Hoot !!!
Yellowstone National Park 1926
Amazing photos and diary written by the author's twenty-six year old mother, Violet Hansen as Violet drove cross-country – 1926.

HISTORIC FICTION

For Love Of Country - A Patriot's Passion
Risorgimento!
Italy 1848–1859
Legend of Italian Patriots in their fifteen-year struggle with General Garibaldi to free, and unify Italy.

The author of this book is an artist, musician, poet, lover of woods, history, people, kittens, Winnie Pooh Bear, a wife, mother, once an educator. I now write full time, and some stories in this collection are personally experienced. Others were told to me. Some are pure fantasy born of events. In most names have been changed with the exception of family history. *And this being the only page that is all about thinking — r*ead on and *e*njoy, finding words to like, or not. *Anyway, mostly words,* and, I must admit, mostly mine, or gratefully borrowed from others who lived these stories with . . .

                                Love, Laughter and Tears. **—*LIZZY***

> A scholar named Wang
> Laughed at my poems.
> The accents are wrong,
> He said,
> Too many beats;
> The meter is poor,
> The wording impulsive.
>
> I laugh at his poems,
> As he laughs at mine.
> They read like
> The words of a blind man
> Describing the sun.
>
>   —*Han-shan – Mystical poet.*
>   *The Tao of Pooh.*

This special collection is dedicated to
My beloved granddaughter

Kate

On our Diamond Anniversary
I gift this to my husband

Floyd L. Downs

Who in the joys of a living love,
Gives me wings of gladness,
And lends my spirit song!

POETRY

- A Treasure
  Carry On.
  Come Walk With Me
  Daybreak
  Diddle - Diddle – Do
- He Walks Beside Us
  I'll Remember You
  In The Wink Of An Eye
  Jingly – Jingly – Jing
  Just Sheer Will
- Loving You
  ! Lies !
  Mr. Bullfrog Will
  Night Closes Tightly
  On Main Street
  One Day
  Pink Petals For Mimi
  Remembering
  The Birth Of A Poet
  To America
  The Awakening
- You Are My Friend
  You Are With Me Still
  What Love Is This
  Winter's Fury
  Woodland Goddess

© *A Spoonful of Sugar.*
• *Dedicated poem.*

STORIES

That Damn Crow	1
Morning Duel ……...………..	11
Bear Country ……..………..	15
Thirst for the Wild ……..….	23
Little Green Prince …..….…	29
Watermelon Summer …....….	35
Old Joe the Hermit ….......…	45
Tornado! …………….....…	55
Racing Red River ………..…	65
Pants ………………..…….	75
Bitter Blizzard ……….….…	83
Poor Bill ……………….…..	95
Love's Reunion …………….	105
Gallery ……………………..	113
Loving Bridget …………….	121
Captain Anton Berntsen …….	129
The Elephant's Trunk ……….	141
The Sixth of June …………..	153
Great Aunt Martine …………	169
Countessa and a Carpenter …..	183

A Novella.

***Little* . . . LIZZY**
The mind reflects and words compel,
On fluted leaves and paper birch,
Between the cabin and the bay.

COME WALK WITH ME

Come walk with me tonight, my friend,
Across these soft, warm desert sands,
Beside the snow capped mountain peaks,
In flickering candlelight,
Here in the midst of scented heather,
Just for tonight, if need be—
Come walk with me, my Friend.

We'll take the gentle, swaying pathway,
Of luminaria that warm the soul,
Past glowing, flaming rooftops,
That guide our footsteps home.

Oh, come walk with me,
Hand in hand,
Just for tonight, if need be—
Find strength in our togetherness,
Share words of hope and love,
Spread Your peace and understanding,
To light the morn of all tomorrows.

Love, Laughter and Tears . . .

THAT `DAMN´ CROW
For Richard . . .

***Willow Hollow* . . . CABIN 1936**
In northern woods it rose,
With grandpa's love,
A cabin of great brown logs,
Still to stand by sky blue water.

THAT `DAMN´ CROW!

It was a gentle rain. When I rolled over to listen, a soft pattering of drops told me the shower was ending. The night had been sticky—warm. And around me the cabin was silent. Pushing the sheet from my feet, I swung out of bed to stand at my window gazing into darkness and treetops . . . drinking in the welcomed coolness. Sunrise would come late on such a morning. It would be enough to tint the treetops a soft golden glow, but not strong enough to burn off the mists rising from our lake below. A slim, keenly-spry eleven-year old . . . plus three months, I had always *felt born to the woods,* setting off on my own into early dawn . . .

Slipping into shorts and top, I found my old blue Keds and crept down to our cabin's lakefront screen porch before putting them on. Lifting the little hook that fastened the porch screen door. — *Listened.* Stepped outside into a delicious quiet before daybreak . . . a time before night disappears, and the surrounding woods remain under a spell of darkness—*my favorite time.*

Owl was hunting . . . his call sounding from those high, wild bluffs surrounding our meadow behind the cabin. An eerie *"o-o-o. . ."* in the stillness. There came the familiar, raspy, "whisk, whisk" of golden birch curls singing against paper birch trunks . . . a dripping sound from fragile leaves glistening with rain. The wetness lifting a mossy scent from the woods, a heavy scent of intoxicating musk—

And I stood feeling it all . . .

Walking slow, I took a downward sloping path through the birch trees, treading *Indian-silent* toward our secluded bay of a small lake in Minnesota's north woods. Cool mist was curling, lifting gently from the water, mist spilling over rocks and shore, to seep into woods, wisps of whiteness on my path. A wet 'thud' of rain hit my head . . . another . . . and with a "swoosh . . . !" came a whole leafy-shower! —I stepped into the open. Soon, *properly damp*, I stood at the shore . . . *listening* . . .

I listened for a familiar, "Caw, caw, caw!" of a very particular crow. A crow my brother Richard had the audacity, *and questionable pleasure,* of naming 'That Damn Crow' some summers before. And even then Crow must have been quite old. It had been coming since the cabin was built—came before the light of day to sit in a great Norway pine that rose beside Richard's second-story bedroom window. And not just any morning, but *every* morning. It was a beautiful bird. One of the largest of crows. And what attracted it to that particular tree the crow never told me, but I thought I knew. that crow seemed to like people . . . *especially my brother.* Why else would that crow pick only Richard's bedroom window to sit beside?

I once asked it:

"Do long needles offer more protection, Mr. Crow?" Then— "Do those cones ooze sweetness, harbor insects you like, Mr. Crow?"

I wondered every time I saw that bird settle into branches it considered its own. And although 'That Damn Crow' never answered me—I waved "Hello" when passing the Norway.

But the crow . . . it just tipped a smooth head, cocked one eye at me and stretched a wing. It knew me—oh yes! Sitting protected in the Norway pine it preened sleek, black feathers over and over with a long, black beak until they shone like patent leather. Then settled, groomed, perhaps fed, Crow would wait. The amazing tenacity of that crow being something difficult to believe, when . . . "Caw, caw, caw!" *began at daybreak of every* morning, *of every* day, *of every* summer without fail. Unless of course, it rained. Then Crow waited—sat huddled against the branches, a black, soggy lump.

But now the rain had stopped. I stood waiting. And 'That Damn Crow' began what it came for:

"*Caw, caw, caw! Caw, caw, caw!...*"

shattered the morning silence

With the cabin on a rise, the huge Norway was visible from the lakeshore offering a sense of security, and I usually started back to the cabin when I heard that first *"Caw, caw, caw!"* from the Norway. So I was retracing my way when suddenly—

I was not alone!

A thin, angular figure stood up there in heavy shadows beside the cabin. Its unmoving stance warned —DANGER!

I felt a pang of fear. No one else could be up so early!

Stepping behind a clump of birch for protection I peered around to decide my next move. We had black bear, *but that was no bear.* Sometimes tramps, once even stray cows, had found their way down into our back meadow . . . but . . . *something told me—*

Don't move!

There were leaves in my mouth. *Push some aside to see better, try to stand motionless,* I warned myself. The figure that stood in those distant shadows was between me and the screen porch door I'd left un-hooked, and I was much too much in the open to circle 'round the cabin without being seen.

"So watch," I told myself.

And the shadow moved . . . moved slowly . . . ever so stealthily into a blotchy patch of first light . . . *a human figure?*

Richard?

From the size, especially what he was wearing—*I knew it was Richard!* "What's he doing out here in those awful pink and green pajamas?" I whispered into some leaves. I knew my brother well . . . *he'd hate being seen in those awful things!* It was difficult, but I held back an urge to shout. Richard was sixteen, five years older than me—I didn't *dare* do such a thing—not at such a moment.

And I had to admit it . . . curiosity had hold of me . . .

"Caw, caw, caw! . . . " had ceased.

I looked. `That Damn Crow' was still there. A big black crow was perched in the middle of the Norway pine, but no "caw" from it. I could see the bird there—tail up—watching the boy below his tree. *Then I'd lost sight of Richar*d. Inching my way, moving from one large stand of birch to another, I got to where I could see both him and the crow. I hugged myself:

Mr. Crow, I bet you woke him up again? Then I said to myself, "Now you're in for it! Richard can be up to no good. Go-on—git!" I began concentrating very hard on that crow, trying to get it to leave.

Something glinted in the light. A gun barrel lifted from beside the pajamas—then went down. I put both hands over my ears. In that early morning stillness a gun-blast would resound like thunder. My parents in their upstairs bedroom, were in for a surprise—

I waited . . . Richard waited . . .

"Crow, you have to get out of there—go, go, go," I pleaded under my breath.

Crow turned its head. Tail up—it wasn't moving. Not one "caw" came out of that bird. —It knew I was watching.

Get out of there crow . . . my inner-self shouted!

Now `That Damn Crow' refused to look at me. Crow never took its eyes off Richard. It was like:

". . , Girl, don't bother me I know what *I'm doing, and right now . . . "*

I took a second, shallow breath, *something had to happen.* I'd been well aware of the feud between the two of them. Crow had always won. *Admittedly, I'd always thought that was great!*

The gun barrel went up again. Richard had crouched down in the dirt.

...Must a' been figuring out his angle, I was thinking. And I wanted to shout, W*hat's the matter with you Crow—fly! Richard's a good shot with that gun!*

"Ca...wk..."

Crow moved to full height of the Norway without lifting a wing. From there, `That Damn Crow´ took flight over Richard's head, curving sharp left. And black wings full out—Crow beating, beating air—rose high over the trees... flew with furious energy—headed out over the lake:

"Caw, caw, caw!..."

—Crow circling 'round, Crow headed back to land...

The last I saw wa*s* a black blur "high tailing" it over trees and hill beside the cabin. `That Damn Crow´ was headed straight for the high, wild bluffs that surrounded the meadow where a steep, two-track road rose out of our land:

"Caw, caw, caw!..."

—Teased back at Richard.

Two red-yellow pajama legs flashed up the hillside and into the woods, *Richard running!* In a crouch he ran, gun in one hand at knee level, other hand pushing branches. —*A true hunter.*

And...I gasped...*Barefoot...!*

I followed—ran fast as I could past the cabin making for the meadow, and trying not to show delight in the chase should my brother turn and see me. But Richard was intent upon `That Damn Crow´. And the crow was in full control of the situation:

"Caw, caw, caw! Caw, caw, caw!..."

—Floating back over the trees. It sounded as if Crow knew it too.

Richard and that crow were going to have it out between them ...*I just knew it!*

Scanning the meadow, I chose a willow tree for watching and ducked under the branches. Then craning my neck—peering up . . .? I could see those pajamas! Richard had made his way to the crest of the bluffs high above me, and far to the left of the top of our road.

Gun at the ready, Richard was placing one foot at a time . . . carefully . . . quietly . . . slowly. I could see how determined he was to get that crow, and I was thinking . . . *poor crow!* When I saw Richard stop. He bent down? He looked up?

—Richard looking to his left . . .

I watched... I could see the crow. Richard's `Damn Crow´ had landed in a high, thick bramble bush not more than twenty-some feet from that gun:

"Caw, caw, caw! . . ."

—Crow was laughing . . .

Richard flattened to the ground—!

"Caw, caw, caw! . . ."

Richard was crawling . . . flat down . . . crawling . . . pushing knees and arms . . . pushing the gun ahead of him. Slowly, slowly he wiggled his way under bushes . . . wiggling, wiggling . . . pushing . . . pushing his gun. Richard making his way under bushes toward Crow.

—Crow sat watching:

"Caw, caw, caw! . . ." Crow snickers.

I knew my brother was mad as anything. And with my feet feeling wet through the Keds, I moved to the bottom of the road . . stared upward . . . Richard? He's out of sight. *No shot. No sound.* I could see Crow—tail in the air—watching. *Still not a sound . . .* **then:**

"Caw, caw, caw! . . ."

—Exploded over the meadow—

`That Damn Crow´ was gone!

Richard? I stared upward . . . where are you Richard? Where is he . . . ? !

Bushes were shaking—*a furious* shaking! One bare foot shot out above those bushes! Then another! Two bare feet began spinning, whirling like propellers, and suddenly Richard shot out from under! Swung right? Swung left! *—A horrible YELL—!*

He took off running . . .

A great crashing of trees, bushes, brush, twigs, is sounding . . . rolling on and on up there across the top of the bluff ! *Suddenly—*

There! *At the top of the road!* That mass of leaves, mud, twigs everywhere! *—Richard?* Richard is high above me! *Going 'round . . . 'round. Wild*-eyed . . . *staring*! He's swinging!

—A powerful roar:

"AAH. . . A. . . G. . . G. . . G . . . ! "

And he's coming!

Richard! Down he's coming! . . . Down, down . . . long strides fighting the fearsome steepness . . . bare feet pounding! *Down, down Richard's coming!* Twigs, dirt, mud, leaves flying! Buttons gone, pajama top flapping . . . *he's coming!*

Down, down, down! Careening! Swinging! Gun in one hand, one arm going 'round . . . around fighting balance! *Down, down he's coming!* Richard—enraged, a rampant fury . . .

And straight at me!

I can't move! Who could move! Transfixed . . . I have no time to even wonder . . . road carrying him straight at me! Racing! Pounding by without a glance. . . . Richard muttering—*muttering*:

"That Damn Crow! . . .

"Damn crow knew that skunk was under those bushes!
 Surprised skunk too! Skunk went one way,
—*Me the other!*

". . . That Damn Crow!"

DAYBREAK

The morning air is standing still,
But a freely running, bubbling brook,
Wanders here, wanders there—
Seeks the goldenrod's secret nook.
Oh to wake after breath of night,
To a calm, refreshing morn,
Where the rushing brook is a pretty sight,
And a springtime day is born.

MORNING DUEL
So it was . . .

SUNRISE
Billowing – bountiful,
Summer clouds.

Photograph: The John Noyes Downs Collection

MORNING DUEL

Golden branches of willow bush swing gracefully over waters of the bay – sway to every wind teasing foam from a rocky shore. And there, in the midst sits Jaybird. A bird so brilliant in blueness, its feathers shine as gemstone beside the golden blossoms. And Jaybird waits. Patient. Watchful. Jaybird waits. Jaybird waiting for *Soft Mist* to lift from northern waters.

But *Soft Mist*, meandering, lingering, is busy dew–kissing Norway pine . . . *a mist* content to let soft whiteness gather hints of sunrise... *Sun* to rise a mysterious phantom.

Sun, mist–hidden, slow to rise, fills damp woodlands with its glow . . . promising no warmth for pristine waters. *Sun* ignoring a Jaybird—first light playing instead, on liquid fingers seeking purple crayfish in rocky fissures of the shore.

So Jaybird waits . . . waits and preens its feathers.

Snake too, waits, assured of breakfast . . . waiting there beneath the willow. Snake so poised and ever silent. Snake a coiled, cold, liquid blackness beneath cobalt-blue berries on purple stems. With deadly grimace, eyes unblinking, Snake is watching—watches—waits for slight of carelessness.

And Jaybird smoothes its feathers.

But *Sun* impatient, proclaims full–majesty, sending forth fearsome, sudden glory—exposing Snake . . . Snake that curls upon itself. Hungry Snake gliding now through scented leaves, seeking safe and dusky woodlands . . . *and*—

Jaybird laughs a raucous laugh to split the morning's silence.

JUST SHEER WILL

Blue—
The sky is heavenly blue,
And Silent,
The wind Strong,
Bare trees rocking, swaying,
Hope—
There is always hope,
Like a glimmer of sun,
Breaking through shadows,
There is hope and Courage,
And Will—
Or perhaps - just sheer will.

BEAR COUNTRY
Courage personified . . .

Wild . . . **BLACK BEAR COUNTRY !**
With huffing, snorting,
Jaw – popping sounds!

BEAR COUNTRY

He saw it too late. The bear rose up from beside the road perhaps as surprised as he was. It was a big one! He judged some 300 pounds of bear, maybe more, and nearly five feet tall on all fours. Now up on its hind feet . . . *height over nine for sure, and way too close for comfort.*

He had taken the side dirt road on the way back to the lake to try out his new bicycle, and had been too complacent, un-watching in bear country . . . , but he had never seen a bear around here. He'd only known from his dad that bear were in the vicinity as it was blueberry season. Now he had one. And it was a big one. And it was right in front of him. *And it had his scent.*

Eagle Scout survival training flooded back . . . *don't move fast - back up slow and get out of there!* But that didn't include a new bicycle. Also, it was five miles back to town,

—He estimated fast.

That meant he was still 30 miles from the lake cabin. And he was on a side road away from the highway—no traffic—no one else around, only woods and total silence. All he heard was a few crows. If he swung the bike around would it bring the bear? *Why was it just staying put? It hadn't moved at all.*

He could put his bike down and retreat, but the bike would be in the middle of the road—*no bike—not smart.* And he'd have his back to a bear—biggest Minnesota black bear he'd ever seen. All this had taken only a few seconds to flash through his mind . . .

Then he saw the cubs. The two cubs were feeding in the woods behind. Now the bear turned into *a she-bear! And with cubs! The most dangerous kind!*

One step back—the bike beside him pushing sand.

Another step . . . pulling the bike with him.

It wasn't a heavy bike. It was one of the new ones built for speed and it had cost his folks a lot. He'd try to keep the bike. It would let him move fast once he had a chance. And unarmed, he thought the bike might be his only safety, *if he could keep it between him and the she-bear.* —Not much, but some safety . . .

Maybe . . .

The she-bear had dropped to all fours, but still hadn't moved. He took several more steps back. The bear didn't move, but she never took her eyes off him. *Scared!* He'd been in scary situations before but never known such fear as this in all his sixteen years. "Don't show fear..." the Eagle manual had warned—

How do you do that . . . he wondered?

Several more steps back. He kept going—pulling the bike. Moved in slow motion. Still no sound of anyone being nearby. *Just crows.* The only way he could go was past the bear unless he wanted to move like this all the way back to where he'd left the highway. He kept going. Kept backing up.

The bear moved.

He took a deep breath—gripped handlebars to stop shaking.

Watching her turn back toward the cubs *he knew she was well aware of him.* He also knew she could move really fast and was powerful. He'd seen the stuffed black bear in an entrance to a bank in Hibbing, Minnesota and it stood some ten-feet of power and fury, with long teeth and huge claws. —He shuddered.

Could he turn around? He wanted to turn around. *Was it safe to turn around. . .?*

That was when he saw it . . .

The dirt road ran along the foot of a low mountain covered by Forest, *but that looks like it might be a trail?*

Moving backwards. Slowly. Pulling the bike. He stood a moment studying what looked like a cut up the mountain through the trees?

A fire–break? Like a trail it looked about five feet wide, and from what he could see it ran to the top of the mountain.

Would it go down the other side? He knew the land well and guessed that on the other side he should find the Sand Lake road . . . *and help.* His eyes found the bear—

She hadn't taken her eyes off him.

But he felt far enough back to move. Waited. Studied the trail upward . . . small rocks. A few big ones. And he could see it was steep . . . *but not too overgrown?*

So he could either wait for the bear to leave the road—*maybe several hours?* Or he could keep walking backwards to the highway, provided the bear let him go . . . and be in the dark by then . . . and miles from the cabin . . . *or* . . . *he could take that trail.* He stared up at the mountain.

So he'd chance it . . .

Moving slowly to the side of the road he waited. Looked for the she-bear... She had moved into the woods with the cubs and was out of sight. But he knew the bear was close to the road. *Probably watching him.* The bear was moving north where he had wanted to go . . . before she'd stopped him. He breathed easier. The bear should be a good distance from the trail.

Lifting the bike, he managed to get it sideways onto his back, and it wasn't too bad. Step after step he started up the trail. Had to put the bike down a couple times to rest, but once he'd made up his mind he kept going . . . shifted the bike onto one shoulder. Somewhere he thought he'd read that bears were territorial? Maybe in the Scout manual?

It made him think.... Maybe if he could get far enough away from the she-bear, he wouldn't have to worry about another bear for quite a ways. *Maybe . . .*

The trail turned out to be a firebreak. Now he was sure of it when at the top of the mountain he could see the trail continuing across a ridge to the north. So ahead of him . . .? It went straight down—!

And going down—slipping, sliding, digging in, was tricky, even when the ground gave firm footholds . . .

Anyway—he wasn't going to go back . . .!

Now all he could do was to keep going down and find out where he'd end up. Looking at his watch he'd been gone some four hours . . . and his folks will start worrying in another hour.

At the bottom of the mountain the trail ended in the midst of granite boulders. Huge boulders as high as his shoulders. One had a flat top, and he climbed up to look around . . . *if he was lucky, he'd see something he knew.* The sun was going down behind some trees ahead and now he could see a dirt road. The road was close. Still further—*was that a lake?* He was pretty sure. *But nothing seems familiar.*

Climbing down he pushed the bike, lifted it up over a steep bank onto the dirt road and scrambling up after it, stood looking around . . .

Where was he?

That's a lake through the trees . . . but he didn't recognize it. No sign of habitation—no lights anywhere—no cabins.

Silence . . .

Then looking to his right down the dirt road . . .?

He could just make out a small brown building about a mile north . . . *does something about that seem familiar?* Could it be the Sand Lake Store . . .?

Maybe . . . but if it is the store, it will close!

Forcing away being tired, the woods were growing dark . . . *but that dirt road was still in pretty good light . . .*

Getting back on the bike he began peddling—peddling hard on the old dirt road. And soon, instead of silence . . . *cars? He was hearing cars!*

. . . There's a highway in front of that building!

Tired, covered with dust, dirt and mud, feet sore in thin sneakers, he figured he was still six miles from their cabin when he got to the store... Climbing the steps he pulled open the screen door, stepped inside and identified himself, then asked the very surprised owner for a dime:

". . . to call my dad."

That brought immediate results from his relieved father who said he'd be there in fifteen minutes.

And the owner—amazed at his story of the bear . . . of a boy walking over that mountain! "And with a bike . . .!"

The owner gave him a free bottle of coke—*and with a straw.*

And taking the bottle outside, Mark sat down on the steps and began sipping. The coke was cool and welcomed.

Getting to his feet, he stared back at the mountain thinking it looked huge and dark in the fading light. *Would anyone believe he climbed that with a bike on his back?*

And he wondered if the she-bear and cubs were safe? She had been a big one.

He didn't care to find out.

 A WISE MAN

"Woods have the power to humble us,
Remind of our place on this planet,
To inspire us . . ."
Said a wise man once who told of
Whispering . . . talking trees.
—

Ah, had we but met you then,
Henry David Thoreau.

THIRST FOR THE WILD
It's in all of us . . .

***River* . . . RAPIDS**
For half-a-mile the river pounds,
Tumbling over sculptured rocks,
With crystal spray - flowing mists.
Cooling sweet the land.

THIRST FOR THE WILD

I feel the pull of northern woods ever so strong in Spring. I felt it that May when I went to the 'hunting camp' . . . so we called it . . . and so it was—a shack used only for hunting. I had just graduated from college, had returned to spend time in the woods I so loved; only to find my family's log cabin sold. From the age of three to eighteen—early June to mid–September—I had lived in those north woods beside a small, glacier-hewn lake; a silent lake to explore at dawn in my Old Town Canoe. Now having returned, I knew it would be my last opportunity to live again, the renewing spirit of the woods. In a few short weeks I would be on my way . . . a new life waiting, the Korean war raging. Still the woods called to me—

It had been a winter of deep snows, and driving north I wondered what I would find. And to my pleasure the little, rugged, shack was in pretty good shape, only one room of wood and shingles, with bunk beds and iron potbelly stove. Beside the stove a stack of wood and kindling was waiting. Here is a small piece of mankind that does not intrude into nature's world. All was in pretty good order except for a smelly mouse nest in the kindling, another nest on a shelf. *Per usual!*

The shack is in woods beside a river that flows north toward Canada's border from a large lake in the northern reaches of Minnesota. This is where the river flows into a shallow gorge with an explosion of rock-torn rapids, a half–mile of pounding waters tumbling over great boulders, sending forth icy sprays of mist to fill the air, keeping the land damp and cool all summer. The rapids never freeze in winter. They are too strong. The shallow gorge is topped by smooth slabs of granite that lay over the land as a flat table-land. Here is where the hunting shack is, close to these granite slabs, deep in the woods only a stone's throw from the river. To get there from a dot on the map a lonely dirt road turns off the highway to Canada heading forty-five miles northwest. You can't drive up to the hunting shack, so everything has to be carried in and out on an over–grown trail, kept wild and unmarked. The shack has no electricity, phone, or running water. The result of all this, I knew, was an enveloping quiet that floats softly down around, washing away all noise and clatter of the world outside, replacing such with the pounding of rapids, peace of woods . . . rare and deeply healing.

I had pulled my car far off road under low sheltering branches, un-sheathed, slipped shells into my rifle, pushed the safety. *Not much against a bear,* but a necessary precaution. Then hefting book, camera, binoculars, a good flashlight, all rolled into my sleeping bag, and a light food pack, I was ready. The fresh fragrance of woods was my first greeting. Crows the second with a chorus of caws from the highest pine trees, followed by a flushing of partridge from the narrow trail. Everywhere trees and woods show early spring growth. Wild yellow buttercups and arbutus, always the first to appear, growing in patches of sun. Bumblebees already busy . . . a *surprise*. But it was too early for whippoorwills and robins, yet I could see a kingfisher fishing from a rock in the center of the river, and a large, gray squirrel scurried from fallen pinecones and leaves.

When I enter the shack that mouse makes it out the door—*a blur*. Some years before a bear had ripped half a corner off our little shack. After that no odors have been left to tempt them, and there is no evidence of bear. *To my relief.* Nor at the privy some ways up a side path. And I bring no meat with me.

Walking across the largest of the flat table-rocks I sit looking down at the rapids, and eating my sandwich. Close across the river a doe and her fawn have stepped from the woods, remain there above the river. As I watch, the doe nudges her young fawn back into shadows. Stands herself ever watchful, absolutely still except for the turning of her head. *She must see me?* But gives no notice. *What does she think of me here?* Then she is gone. With only that white flash of tail, leaving me with a memory of something beautiful. Two very small chipmunks make me turn, grinning, to watch them scrambling through fallen leaves with chip - chip – chattering, white stripes and tails quivering. Seeming so busy. Ignoring me.

There is early spring everywhere. And I feel it as I take a path along the river. Wildflowers in the sun here are just beginning to bud. They will be a blaze of color soon with the river's dampness, and on hot summer days. I recognized some: foxtail, the red of Indian paintbrush, the milkweed, but some I don't know.

"…It is heart–warming, really, this hunger and thirst for the wild. It is in all of us…" so said Yeats – *and so it is* - as I make my way to the river to stand on a great boulder, enjoying the icy spray. There is a huge rock out in the middle if one is brave enough. Not I. Hearing the waters roar past me is enough to renew my hope that nothing will destroy this wonder. Certainly something I have missed, and will carry life-long..

Before dusk I finally hear the great loons, friends since long-ago paddling my Old-Town canoe. Now I am listening to their pensive calls echo across the stillness, *a sound like no other.* There is a place on table-rocks for fires, but I will only sit here eating my supper. This time with strong coffee, slabs of white cheese. And I will turn-in early before nightlife begins to wander.

At first light I stand watching the sun color tips of fir on the other side of the river, hear the woods whisper as they come awake. Having learned as a child to let solitude talk to me, that an inner sensitivity to the nature of things. After four days at the shack I left with myself renewed – appeased for a while. *- LIZZY.*

THE AWAKENING

A love of woods and nature,
Their still small voices call,
Awakening man's true inner nature,
Seeing things about ourselves,
We need to get rid of,
Those things we need to change,
A mind that sees what lies before it,
Follows the nature of things,
Maybe an empty sort of mind . . .

LITTLE GREEN PRINCE
So . . . tell me why . . .

The . . . **WATERS ARE LONELY**
Where once you swam,
My little prince,
The mind rebels . . .

Photograph: The John Noyes Downs Collection.

LITTLE GREEN PRINCE

In the northern regions of Minnesota between Duluth and International Falls there existed not long ago many native aquatic species where cliffs are ancient and bold, waters of glacial lakes deep and blue. A blue that reflects the sky. It is a land of bitter winters and great beauty. A land of forests meeting waters' edge, of narrow, agate–strewn beaches.

And close upon such a beach, in the secluded bay of a small lake, is the log cabin of Honoré. There she and I lived in childhood, and there Honoré returns every summer. So I immediately thought of my friend when I read about the tiny spotted frog, knowing she would soon return to the lake. *and . . .*

Honoré eagerly accepted my petition as her personal mission: *"Find a little green prince."*

Creatures of woods and water had been our youthful playmates, mine and Honoré's. To the tiniest of frogs we had given the tribute: *"Little Green Prince,"* for it had gifted us with much pleasure. Its sleek, lime–green body with black spots and slender waist was the pinnacle of graceful elegance. Long legs double–folded against smooth sides proved agility unrivaled—the species a glistening joy no longer than my little finger—*exquisite.* Asking only to live. Therefore my request of Honoré.

And from the cabin she wrote:

..."*At first arrival I was sure of a little green prince whose soprano voice leads an evening chorus beneath my window, but in the past month I have not seen even one. Early this morning a soft spring mist rolled over the waters of this easternmost bay when I made my way to the shore. I felt the soft breath of dampness upon my cheek, and somewhere, creatures scurried through the fading night. Dear friend, —my heart beats all the more swiftly in anticipation.*" —**Honoré**.

I realize now her words intensified my anxiety. I remembered how clear blue eyes glistened above strong Nordic cheekbones in an elderly face. I knew that wind-tossed wisps of gray hair would be pushed away with an impatient hand as Honoré waited. Will he come? I wondered?

The answer was somewhere within Honoré's second letter:
..."*I have waited—I still wait—now with growing concern for our little green prince. The waters, once clear—translucent to so great depths—are muddy. I have never seen weeds rise over the waters before. Somewhere a pump is working in marshlands where great blue heron fish and loons nest. Draining for houses. With daylight the roar of seaplanes shake my woodlands and speeding boats race across the big bay to the west—shattering—destroying the morning's fresh scent. Still, I remain hopeful.*" —**Honoré**.

With her next letter I recalled how waters push into calm eddies between the rocks along that shore, how crawdads, minnows, tiny black tadpoles, scurried at will in the liquid pools. But there was no evidence of a tiny green prince.

Still, Honoré believed he would come—that he must come:
..."*I have waited so long—he must be somewhere!*" she wrote. "*From under my feet a giant bullfrog flung himself into the bay with a heavy 'Plunk' of ever-expanding rings. Every living thing scurried. Every minnow out of sight . . . 'I'm sorry fella!' My whispered apology received a silent stare... 'Gr-umph, gr-umph'* – *a ponderous sound, resonance deep and mellow... 'Gr-umph, gr-umph, grump!' The white*

softness of his throat spoke defiance. Masterful kicks took him further out where sunlight cast warmth upon the waters. Handsome, bold, he turned to glare at me. Blink. Blink . . . one eye at a time. Still —no sign of the little green prince." —**Honoré**

May to September Honoré rose, slipped out of the cabin so silently when woods and waters were still asleep. But the tiny frog was gone long before. She knowing then, it would not ever be there:

. . ."*And a great sadness rose to tears,*" she wrote. "*So it was not he that sang at night. I had been mistaken . . . my bony finger in the cold water only brings his sweet memory closer.*" —**Honoré**

With these words from Honoré I know it was true what my journals told me—what we could not believe—would not believe—had gone so far to disbelieve. In reality, the tiny Green Spotted Frog was indeed extinct. Gone from the face of the earth—absolute. Extinct from the scarcity of oxygen-giving waters and habitat? I inspect comments in periodicals—search in vain. With callous indifference a growing blight upon our planet, such a tiny life couldn't matter. And I wonder if the giant bullfrog, blinking, blinking—knew *fear*—was staring at his own extinction.

In October, cold winds moved south from Hudson's northern bay, and crisp leaves whirled to her path as Honoré penned a last note from the cabin:

. . ."*I will soon leave. All the birds have flown, I miss our little green prince.*" —**Honoré**

I experience with those words, a passion rich with memories —empty feelings of senseless loss. There are those who tell us it is inconsequential . . . who tell me a tiny frog contributed nothing. But I think of its rare beauty. I think of marshlands with pink lilies, the great blue heron and great loon; sunfish, crawdads, the curious dragonfly— woodlands, blue jays and meadowlarks; the bobolink and robin—black bear and green striped garter snake. *What of them?* The mind recoils at the thought.

—Extinct 2003, "The Tiny Green Spotted Frog."

MR. BULLFROG WILL

"Tell me please, Auntie Flo,
So wise . . . so wise . . .
What's that bullfrog a' saying?
The one I hear so in the night,
That bullfrog I calls - Mr. Will."

―

"Campbell Soup – Good Soup!
My darlin'," says she . . .
"Campbell Soup – Good Soup!
Campbell Soup – Good Soup!
That's what that bullfrog's a'saying."

WATERMELON SUMMER
Incredibly, truly true . . .

***Oh!* . . . JULIETTE**
Pretty Julie . . . slim and spry,
Nineteen with history to make . . .
Never to be surpassed!

WATERMELON SUMMER

"Echoes over water really do sound strange . . . " was his first thought . . .

Mike stopped short . . . held his balance in the shallow water. He'd been bending over searching between rocks for craw-dabs. Now he stood up. Waited. And the sound came again. Rebounding from a hillside near the cabin the shout skimmed toward him over the waves:

"Ka–thy. . . he—l—p!". . .

In all his nine years of living Mike had never heard anything like that cry as it came at him in pieces. But that was his mother's voice. He was sure. And to Mike *a cause for panic:*

"Ka–thy . . . he–l—p!"

He made it to the beach in a wild splashing run, and ignoring bare feet, took a short cut through the pines, made a quick pass up a slope to the screen porch, and leaping two steps—flung the door wide . . . left it to slam on its own. Right behind came cousin Julie—

"*Kathy!*" Sounded again.

Kathy, a young woman hired to help with the new baby, had barely beaten Mike through the kitchen archway when his wet feet hit the linoleum floor and he came to a skidding stop in the midst of oranges, apples, potatoes, rutabagas, lemons . . . a head of cabbage . .

finally toppled into a massed heap of grocery bags. *Bags everywhere! Bags on the kitchen floor—bags on counters—paper bags every which way...Bags! Bags! Bags!*

Struggling to his feet, *shaken* . . . Mike was utterly bewildered. Obviously, his mother had driven the forty-some miles to town for groceries, *but—*

"Mrs. Jeffries? Vi . . . ?" Kathy looked around in wonder.

"*Kathy!* Oh thank goodness!"

Violet's voice rose a great *whooshing–pant* from the far side of a humongous, black iron cook-stove that squatted on fat, bulbous legs taking up one whole wall of the cabin's little kitchen. And peering around it—Kathy stood perplexed, not daring to go closer.

Violet, legs akimbo, was sliding, banging back-and-forth . . . *whooshing . . . panting . . .* her arms in a death-defying grip around a huge, formidably heavy, wooden dumbwaiter.

As amazed as Kathy, Mike stared—*speechless.*

Their summer cabin in these north woods had no electricity. That dumbwaiter was supposed to be suspended by ropes in a well shaft where it could be lowered over an ice-cold well far below the kitchen, to keep their food cool. Mike had never seen it out of that well shaft, but knew it as a large box—five-feet high, about three feet wide, with *front-to-back* three foot sides! Open only at the front, there were five shelves. His grandfather had built it, "Like those in the old country," he'd told Mike, meaning Italy. And Mike knew—of *vital importance—that well was their drinking wate*r.

"*Kathy!.* . . I need you . . ." *wheezed* Violet . . .

Refusing to let go of the dumbwaiter—*that seemed to be winning*—Violet was pushing . . . tugged . . . did a dangerous two–step–pirouette trying to stay upright and not get clobbered!

"But what are you doing, Auntie Vi.?" asked Julie, the first one to come to her senses.

"Watermelon . . . fell in—"

"A watermelon fell into the well! !" Kathy stared unblinking.

"An' . . . Got . . . pull this out," panted Vi... "Won't come."

It was obvious to Mike that his mother was getting the worst of the struggle. But for *its* part, the heavy dumbwaiter—with every swing up—viciously turned—hurtling back into the well shaft *thumping, banging, shaking* the massive, iron cook-stove ridding all open shelves above, clean of anything movable, salt-&-peppers, pots, covers, trays, hot pads, cook spoons . . . clattering down with an echoing, clamoring, racket!

Only Kathy dared get closer.

Moving in, matching Violet's swing and sway, Kathy came dangerously close to the well shaft herself until, even with the two of them tackling the stubborn dumbwaiter—the unruly hulk defeated them.

"I'll get a rope," panted Kathy, "maybe we can pull it over and tie it to the stove leg."

" . . . Good strong one," Violet sank to the floor. "Hurry!"

Julie was already out the door.

"In the woodshed!" Mike led the way, "There's rope in there!"

Then when Mike couldn't reach the hook, it was Julie who raced back with a great length of rope . . .

And grabbing it— Kathy tied the rope to a convenient steel ring on the bottom of the dumbwaiter while Violet looped the other end *twice* around one of the bulbous rear legs of the massive, iron cook-stove . . .

Then— Violet began pulling . . . while Kathy pushed.

Standing open-mouthed Mike watched as—

. . the dumbwaiter's bottom swung up—tipped first left—swung a violent far right—made a slow pass left again, and suddenly gave up! *Gently as you please*—that dumbwaiter just laid over to its right far enough to clear the well shaft. There it hung. Shelves pointing to the ceiling in surrender.

Confident the cook-stove would not budge Violet went to find a flashlight. Then returning . . . everyone crowding around the well shaft was hit in the face by a fierce, chilling up–draft—!

"Oh my Gawd," breathed Kathy.

"Wow . . ." Mike could only *whisper* . . .

Far below, in a faint circle of yellow light, a mass of *jiggly* black water looked forbiddingly deep and cold. And there—right in the middle—bobbed a large green ball.

"The watermelon!" Julie gulped.

"Jeeze look at that," whispered Kathy, "how long do you think it'll float?"

Violet gave a start— "We've got to get it! It'll pollute the whole well!"

"Forty miles from help, and no telephone—and that!" Kathy pointed at the floating melon then swung around . . ."I'll get a rake! Do we have a pitchfork?"

"Maybe… Up in Grandpa's garden I think," Mike sat down to pull on some shoes.

"*No!*" Violet shook her head, "We can't break it open."

"Oh, you're right!" Kathy reconsidered. And taking off on the run for the woodshed she came back carrying a basket lashed to a long tent pole—exclaimed:

"We can fish it out!"

But try as they might . . . the well shaft was *far* too deep.

"If it sinks we're in *real trouble*," Mike's contribution to doom.

"A longer rope," mused Violet, "and stronger. I'll have to go in and get it. . . . I'm skinny enough."

"Mrs. Jeffries? Vi.!" You've just had a baby! I'll have to do it," protested Kathy. And returning from *yet another trip* to the woodshed—this time carrying a coil of thick rope left from hanging the swing in the meadow . . .

Kathy began taking off her clothes…

Shaking her head Violet looked at short, pudgy Kathy, "You know . . . I'll never be able to pull you back out Kathy."

"Oh—" Kathy's laugh was infectious.

Mike couldn't help it . . . *had to giggle* . . . then suddenly cried out, "Maybe we can lasso it, Mom! You know—like Tom Mix!"

"That's it!" Julie's shout turned everyone around—

"I can get it, Auntie Vi! *Lasso me*—tie the rope around my waist—*I can get it*!"

Violet looked at her. She and Kathy looked at each other. They looked back at Julie—spry Julie—thin, barely nineteen-year-old Julie who had those long, strong arms—

"Think so?" Violet bit at her lip.

"I think so." Kathy found it hard *to say anything.*

"Okay."

Mike started to say, "You're crazy—" But he didn't say it. Instead, for once, he decided he'd better keep his mouth shut.

With one end of rope around Julie's waist—between her legs—tied in front of her chest, Violet secured the rope to a second leg of the iron cook-stove. Then with Kathy, she tried tugging it. *They did their mightiest!* And when they were sure . . .

Still in her swimsuit, Julie got onto the edge of the well shaft. She swung her legs over, glanced down into *cold, pitch-blackness* . . . sat *thinking*. Then with both hands gripping the rope in front of her chest, pronounced:

"I'm ready, Auntie Vi—"

Violet turned on the flashlight, c*onsidered* . . . turned and gave it to Mike, "You've got to hold this Mike. And for goodness sake don't drop it . . . !"

So holding a flashlight in two hands, trying not to shake, Mike found himself *peering down at the water,* shining a circle of yellow light on a watermelon.

"Ready," said Violet. She and Kathy braced themselves—

. . . Holding the rope with two hands, Julie was lowered over the edge. There she hung—bare feet pushing against wooden sides of the well shaft—

The rope began to move . . .

Julie's head went out of sight. Peering down after her . . . Violet held her breath—until she finally had to breathe— *"Hiccup!"*

". . . *little lower*—" came a muffled voice from the well.

Mike saw the water move, *saw two arms come into the circle of light*—

"She's got it!"

"I've got it!" came a shout from the well.

"Pull Kathy - **Pull!!** "

Working hand-over-hand Julie's head was brought up to the opening . . . her shoulders . . .

' Splat! '

. . . A cold, wet watermelon landed near Mike's feet, and Julie was pulled into the kitchen a heap of shivering arms and legs—

"Brr...rrrrr . . . it's freezing down there!"

The blanket felt good - Julie hugging it close while Kathy wrapped it three-times around, then sent her out to sit in a patch of sunshine on the back porch. And following to sit down beside her . . . Mike began peeling an orange to share.

Kathy—*limp*—barely made it to the kitchen counter, leaned against it, swallowing twice—snuffed-in breath . . . watched Violet *do* the dumbwaiter . . .

As leaping nimbly to one side Violet untied, and released the dumbwaiter to the well shaft—

. . . Saw it *hurdle down!*

. . . Saw it *stop with a vengeance like thunder—!*

. . . Saw it give three *mighty shudders*—settle *peacefully* . . .

Satisfied, Violet went over to rest beside Kathy. A tall, slim woman, she could lean back resting both elbows behind her on the counter— closed her eyes.

"How'd it ever get down there?" whispered Kathy.

Vi let out a *sigh* . . .

"You'll never believe . . . I was putting the melon on the bottom shelf . . . when that *ding-dong* dumbwaiter did a good swing back and the melon just rolled out—

Down it went! "

Vi looked over at Kathy, "Find it hard to believe, myself..."

"Next time get a square melon," giggled Kathy.

That did it—! Clinging . . . doubling over with fits of laughter, the mingling of tears brought relief.

. . . . .

Decades later when Mike was almost 79 and Juliette had just celebrated her 90th birthday, they were sitting together in Tucson, Arizona one day . . . *when Mike finally asked:*

"You know, Julie . . . what were you thinking of when Mom and Kathy lowered you down into our well—?"

It brought a sly grin . . .

"Mike if you really want to know. . . I expected you to drop that flashlight on my head."

I'LL REMEMBER YOU

Pattering, pattering, a caressing of raindrops,
Upon silken leaves, draws me to the window,
And the pre-dawn shower is gentle . . .
Will taper off at first light, I know.

For such is the way of a summer's rain,
Whispering, whispering, tiny leaves of graceful,
Paper birch are whispering . . .
And I am listening.

Perhaps this sound will remain with me forever,
A pattering, pattering, of gentle drops,
Upon fluted leaves. and I'll take it with me . . .
And I will nurture it.

For when I'm no longer a child, and days are many,
I'll want to feel it again, this soft cool rain,
Listen again to whispering leaves . . .
And I'll remember you.

OLD JOE THE HERMIT
Ode to Mr. Toaster . . .

***Old Joe's* . . . RAIL - CAR HOME**
Two doors to let a breeze inside,
A scent of sweet summer's meadow,
One comfy place!

OLD JOE THE HERMIT

From a high bluff near his homestead Joe can look right over his meadow to forests that stretch as far as the Laurentian Mountains, close beyond lies Canada, even further—Hudson's huge bay. New to America, before 1930 Joe had claimed his homestead beside little Ely Lake in northern Minnesota, when it could only be reached by a foot trail sixteen miles from a small mining town. And few souls knew the foot trail existed. Then came a split–log, rough corduroy road. Now in 1936 a narrow sand road is winding through isolated woods, and curves to run right past Joe's place.

Short and wiry, Joe moves around his big meadow with an up–down–humping motion, more an amble than stride. His skin is sun–baked and weathered. But make no mistake, Joe is all muscle. And everything about him is brown—brown streetcar, brown flannel shirt, brown wool pants and high laced boots . . . maybe all he owns. Except under the flannel shirt is a one–piece, gray wool, union suit with tiny, ivory bone buttons. Joe wears it both summer and winter. If it's a warm day, he takes off his flannel shirt to roll up sleeves of the union suit like Popeye's muscles.

For Joe, a favorite *tabacc*a pipe satisfies, fills the space where some teeth should be. And that pipe's always there—maybe brings a feeling of contentment. Its when he takes it out to speak that the words sort of drift along, become part of Old Joe's charm.

It's that streetcar in Joe's meadow summer–folk stop to stare at. The story going, that the streetcar used to carry miners some thirty miles to work and back on tracks through the woods, yet no one seems to know how it ended up as a house for a Hermit. The metal roof is a patchwork of mending. Every window so pitted from hailstorms Joe can't open them. Instead, two doors let a breeze inside with a scent of sweet summer's meadow–grass and pink clover. And those doors are always open. Joe chose a good spot to settle just beyond gentle hillsides that surround the lake. Peaceful, good water, a meadow warmed by sun–lit mornings, and the rusty–gold of a fall sunset. *Very satisfying place.*

That's how it was when the summer of 1937 began with hot, muggy days. Just the same as always. Except for a lone Ford truck going back and forth on the sandy road lifting a cloud of dust every time it passed Joe's meadow. So Joe. he knows he has a neighbor, a tall Norwegian proud of heritage, by the name of Finn Lundsted, *or some such dang moniker,* Joe thought was strange to the ear. And when friendly Finn Lundsted began calling him "Old Joe," why, Joe took to calling his neighbor just plain—"Finn."

Finn and his wife Gudrid have built them a little cabin two miles away, around three bends in the road, and Finn is settling in to raise billy-goats. Seeing this, Joe begins *neatening up* his place, taking a long–handled scythe to weeds 'round the streetcar and putting up a wire fence beside the road to hold back his chickens. And when Finn sees this, he decides to loan Joe a billy-goat to crop the meadow, and soon the two men are friends.

On those bluffs overlooking the lake three other cabins are being built near Joe—more neighbors.

"Summer–folk," Finn dubs them.

And the name fits, because, except for Mutt–dog, Joe is isolated all nine months of winter. He grins and tells Finn:

"Summer–folk ain't brave 'nough to tempt surviving any of a Minnesota winter with no cold–proof cabin, phone or plow . . . an' no electricity . . . hav'en to melt snow when the well freezes."

Joe had Finn laughing.

"Sure'n toot'en . . . an' it be no indoor plumbing!" roars Finn.

Joe liked that one too, *set him chuckling all that daylong.*

So before the last week of August, water pipes were drained, out–house privies boarded up, canoes, dories, oars and paddles, dragged into sheds . . . then bedding, foodstuffs, kids, cats and dogs, were loaded into cars, and summer–folk were set to disappear. Finn Lundsted, too, had his goats inside before a September frost. But when temperatures fell to *ten above*, and the ground was firming up—froze solid—finally too, Finn and Gudrid were loading their goats into the Ford truck and left until a spring thaw.

But even when red in his thermometer sticks at forty–below and the Lake freezes *'most* to the bottom, Joe is at home in his streetcar. October brings ice. November brings snow drifting high–up against frost–painted windows, and December brings freezing Arctic winds from Hudson's Bay with more snow and ice keeping Joe busy splitting logs for his wood–burning cookstove. Firewood is stacked ground to roof outside like insulation.

The streetcar is toasty warm as all winter long a grey-brown ooze rises from the roof 's stovepipe, hits frigid air and flattens out over the woods like a pancake. And that smoke never seems to get past those gray clouds that hang over the meadow. Clouds pregnant with more snow. So that's when Joe sits back in his old mohair chair, thumb–packs *tabacca* into his pipe . . . waits for a day of crisp, mid–winter sunshine. He's content, Joe and Mutt–dog, and suddenly the streetcar house looks very warm—comfy.

Odd fellow, Finn had wondered to himself when he first met Joe. And summer–folks question between themselves—

"How can Joe survive?"

Then if someone asks . . . why Joe just smiles.
It seems that Old Joe is a character of the sort legends are made, having lived on the lake trail as long as anyone can remember . . .

Our hermit in a streetcar.

And some wonder if there isn't something to envy about Joe the Hermit who roams free as the wind gathering gooseberries, chokecherries, and green–furry hazelnuts. In July, Joe can be seen coming out of the woods with brim-full buckets of crab apples, purple blueberries, mouth–puckering pin-cherries, spitting seeds all the way to his meadow where he tends a garden of potatoes and sweet corn. New piglets every spring give him bacon all winter.

Still, it's summer afternoons Joe is envied for most. That's when he can be found beside his streetcar house, leaning back in an old, wooden kitchen chair, smoking his pipe with Mutt–dog dozing beside him. Chickens scratch here—scratch there—wander the huge meadow without a bother. And if anyone asks?

Why Joe says:

". . . jest restin' the bones."

It was June when the new rooster arrived in Joe's meadow with a raucous *!-cock–a–doodle–do-!* capable of shaking every crow from pine trees for miles around—sunrise to sundown. And things quickly became serious with that rooster taking a dislike of Finn Lundsted. —Downright hatred.

"An' I be down–right wary of chickens!" . . . Finn's words to Joe came out sputtering . . .

"Moreover," Finn admitted, "I'm *specially* scared of this dang new roost–bird you calls Mr. Tooster."

But Joe is proud of Mr. Tooster, a huge white rooster bird with wrinkled orange feet, fiery-red coxcomb and long yellow beak. And soon that rooster rules Joe's meadow with one beady eye—left over from a fight.

And that Mr. Tooster is *downright mean!*

So Joe tells his friend:

"If mad, mad, Tooster puts its head to one side—*puts that evil eye* on you—jest RUN!"

So it was . . . *but—*

Now all Joe's hens were white 'cepting for one very small speckle-gray Mr. Tooster soon takes a fancy to. The big rooster following that little speckle-gray crowing furiously, prancing with wings *a-flustering* and feathers *a–flying* as it chases speckle–gray all over the meadow, giving Joe no peace at all. Yet when summer–folks stop by the fence to laugh . . . why, Joe sells more chickens! He just walks up to folks any fine summer's morning with a warmth in his soft brown eyes that people like.

However, by the mid-of-July, Joe is fed–up . . . is down right angered, *by that Mr. Tooster's shenanigans.* This is especially so one memorable morning when Finn Lundsted happens by with a goat for the meadow . . . *and—*

Climbing down from his old Ford truck Finn exclaims:

"Ya, 'et bird´s coo–coo. Sure be mad—worse´n be ever he is!"

"No controllin' Mr. Tooster," admits Joe. And all of a sudden Joe's thinking, . . . *If I kills that speckled hen? Why it sure will `cure` what ails* that *rooster!* So Joe—right then—he makes a fateful decision:

"Finn, you wants a stew´n bird fer supper?"

And Finn grins, "Sure `nough, it be fine!"

Quick as anything Joe leans down to pick up the speckle-gray, and with one twist he wrings that bird's neck . . . begins to cut off the head on a chopping block—*when something goes awful wrong.* Joe's grip is slipping on the hen . . . and that little speckle-gray she takes off a–flopping–squawking with a strange, funny–like sound. While Mr. Tooster, that bird just goes crazy! Spotting his sweetie running around '*most* headless—the sight drives Tooster berserk.

Finn sees Mr. Tooster take off for speckle–gray—

And there—after the rooster goes Joe . . . a–hollering some incomprehensible language!

"Whoa dere—!" shouts Finn. He makes a beeline for the Ford.

So that bloody hen, she just flips over—honestly—truly dead, and Joe grabs that hen to toss it up on the woodpile . . .

"Hi—Look out 'im!" hollers Finn.

Cured? Oh no, not Mr. Tooster. Not by a-long-shot. Red coxcomb straight up, beak wide-open, a furious Tooster heads for Joe. Wings outstretched, shrieking *!!!cock–a–doodles!!!* a flying Tooster hits Joe *smack-dab* in the middle of his chest where a yellow beak draws bright red blood right through the union suit!

"Yiiee—! You Tooster!" Joe rips out a yell—

He lets go with a boot to kick that bird clear over the wire fence and into the road—*a mighty kick!*

Lots of squawking!

And with Finn having a laughing fit behind the old Ford's fender Joe *begins a hearty chuckling.* He grabs that bloody hen and starts in a-plucking—plucking at all those gray feathers . . .

Flying feathers everywhere!

"Hi—Joe! Look 'et the bird!"

Infuriated, not to be mastered—shaking its hurt pride, comes a dancing, prancing Mr. Tooster up to Finn's truck. And laying its head to one side, that bird turns its beady eye on Finn who makes a mighty leap into the old Ford. Slams the door. Sits pumping up windows—!

Then Finn looks down. *He's staring into one evil eyeball!*

That Tooster's pecking a–rage at the Ford's front tire—raising an awful stink.

"Hi—Joe! Come git the damn bird!" Finn is leaning out, flap–flapping with a rag . . .

"Hi—you roost-bird, git from the tire! Shoo—g'wan—git! g'wan—git! you!!" screams Finn.

"*Aiiee—!* Tooster!" Joe goes for a broom . . .

"Joe! Joe!" hollers Finn, Get your dag–blast–roost! I'm gone run over 'im right sure—NOW!"

"Tooster—!" Broom in hand Joe advances on the rooster—

"Blast–chicken—git–g'wan–git from my tire . . . !"

Finn be throwing paintbrushes, pushing keys trying to fit the ignition, and wild–eyed Mr. Tooster is a–digging out chunks of black rubber—when Joe finally lays into those tail–feathers with a goodly *swat* of muddy broom!

That's just too much for a furious rooster—

Flying through an open door of the streetcar—beating wings against windows front-to-rear—Tooster lets loose with one scorching *!–cock–a–doodle–do–!* after another . . .

And Finn finally hits the gas—

Then . . . it's one mile more to make it to his place, and Finn can still hear that bird . . . *when he's hearing "air too—!"* . . . and the old Ford is limping to a stop. Now Finn Lundsted is swearing to the end of friendship . . .

"Sure is—sure be!"

Come early August . . . it was, when summer–folk realized they hadn't seen . . . nor heard, that big white rooster with one eye and those wrinkled orange feet—not for some time? Nowheres in Old Joe´s meadow? Finally Finn Lundsted stops at Joe´s place..

Finn leans out of the Ford and there is Old Joe . . . Joe sitting in his chair up-against the streetcar house, Mutt–dog beside him.

A bantam's high rainbow tail is moving through wheat grass on the far side of Joe's quiet meadow.

Finn eyes it suspiciously.

Removing his pipe Joe grins at him, "Where ya been?"

"Hey Joe, where's 'et Tooster?"

"Pig got 'im," came the answer—

Finn grinned back, "Ya! Sure . . . could be so."

JINGLY–JINGLY–JING!

It's only three miles to the country store,
A country store with creaky door,
The old screen door of rusty-brown,
Only three miles on a summer's day,
Down a road of pebbly sand . . .
With pennies in a pocket
Going – jingly-jing!
Pennies in a pocket to spend.

It's only a mile past old Joe's place,
A farm and cow with a kindly face,
On a winding road past apple trees,
Meadow of clover with honeybees,
Just a lovely, dreamy way to go . . .
With pennies in a pocket
Going – jingly-jing!
Pennies in a pocket to spend.

It's another mile beyond the hill,
Where bobtail rabbits sit so still,
Beside a pond with bubbly spring,
Walking with a song to sing . . .
With pennies in a pocket
Going – jingly-jing!
Pennies in a pocket to spend.

It's around the bend, one mile more,
Three sandy miles on a summer's day . . .
With pennies in a pocket to spend
Going – jingly–jingly,
Jingly–Jingly–Jing!

! TORNADO !
With Patricia . . .

! TORNADO !
Over forest and water,
Fearsome fate - summer 1968.

Photograph: Eric Lantz, Walnut Grove, MN. June 13, 1968.

! TORNADO !

Nan looked up from her sewing. The wind was rising. She sensed it. Then came a rasping of branches against the back wall of the cabin . . .

Wind always made her nervous. It added to her feeling of being 'put upon' having lived with so many such storms, and being uneasy alone in the woods. Once a bear was out there. A bruin! Coming through the trees! *That was really too much!*

And now this . . . Craig gone for a whole week, and her alone here with the kids. And all five, because . . . "Mom, we just have to stay at the lake!" . . . *So she had stayed.* Tucked away in the woods, the two cabins were isolated. Even so close to the lake, it gave the feeling of being hundreds of miles from town—instead of forty-some. . . . *Made her nervous.*

A night rain had cooled the July morning, but fifteen-year-old Rob had built a fire, and Nan sat listening. The wind was coming up stronger. *She didn't like the sound of it.* Putting her work aside, she walked over to look out the kitchen window at trees, and the large, older cabin that belonged to her in-laws. The pine trees were swaying. She'd never known those large trees could bend so, branches almost sweeping the ground.

She told herself, "When little Andy wakes from his nap she should put the kids in the car and drive to town." . . . *but by then it might really storm and they'd be in it . . .*

That's not sensible. Maybe she'd better stay put.

The girls, nine-year old Lyn and Vickie being eight, played well together. That was a help. Nan looked in on them playing cards, sitting cross–legged on the bottom bunk in their bedroom. Four year-old Andy was asleep on her and Craig's double bed. But Rob and Tom had a mean game of checkers going in front of the fire in the cabin's front room that was both living room and kitchen. And Nan knew there was enough firewood under the over–hang beside the door. So seeing them all content she relented. *They'd stay put.*

Sitting again, looking over at the boys, she found herself smiling. Rob would be a high school junior that fall and had just earned his Eagle. Now she could tell he was winning—flipping checkers—lording it over Tom soon to be thirteen. Their shouts almost drowned out the wind, *how can they ignore so much going on outside?*

And the wind seemed worse. *More and more nervous*, she went back to the little kitchen window, stood looking at her in–laws' cabin . . . *if Craig's parents hadn't stayed in town, she could go over there with the children.* Just then a large floor mat from that cabin's porch blew—went sailing—a heavy rubber mat. Nan stared.

"Mom!"

Rob's shout turned Nan toward the large, plate–glass window facing the lake. *Shaking! The whole window is shaking!*

Alarmed, she ran over to look toward the lake. Saw whitecaps and churning waves. Two thirty-foot pines by the beach were whipping, sand flying. But what Nan saw coming directly at them from across the water stopped her breath . . .

"Tornado—!"

Rob's shout woke Andy. Brought all the children to their feet.

"Coming right at us—!" screamed Tom.

Nan was moving. How she did it . . . where the idea came from, she would never know, but in the next instant she was shouting:

"Under the beds! Everyone! Get under the beds!"

Grabbing Andy, she pulled him with her under the double bed, the girls pushing in beside her. Tall and slim, Nan still struggled to get herself under as far as she could—pulling her feet up. And with her arm around Andy, she lay hugging the floor. *Shouted*—

"Rob! Tom! —Are you okay!"

"We're under the bunk beds!"

Those were the last words Nan heard before a massive whirl of wind hit the beach with a thunderous roar!! The crashing of trees filled her senses— Wood splintering! Bursting! —Shrill screaming trees! Horrendous screaming trees! Lying there, clutching Andy, Nan began praying. Felt the cabin shaking. Cabin shook harder. *Kept shaking. Over a terrifying roar* . . . from somewhere came the sound of shattering glass. The deadly, twisting, howling of wind lessened— finally moved on . . .

Then *silence.*

"Can we move?" Nan turned her head . . . *why am I asking*?

She looked at Lyn's back - the two girls hugging each other. Forcing herself out from under the bed she took Andy's hand and motioned to the girls.

"Rob, Tom, are you okay?"

"Okay! We're coming!"

"Yea—"

One by one they came to stand before the large front window that miraculously was intact. Nan stood trying to see the lake. Those two huge trees near the beach had disappeared or must have been torn to shreds, *she couldn't see them.* She could not see the water. Fallen, twisted tree trunks, massive branches and foliage formed a barrier as high as the other cabin's roof and all the way out to the lake. Nan realized the stone wall before the beach must be gone. The pontoon float too. But from what she could make out, her in-laws' cabin stood firm in spite of being so close to the lakefront.

Then it surprised her to see green shingles on that cabin's roof standing up on end, *the tornado must have lifted from the water and flown over both cabins!*

"Good Lord, thank you," she breathed—

Somewhat stunned, hardly aware of little Andy's arms around her waist . . . Nan slowly became aware of voices. Then words registered—

"It went right over us!"

"What a mess!"

"My God!"

"Right over grandpa's cabin and missed us!"

"Kitchen window's gone—there's glass all over!" *Then—*

"Mom! We can't get out!"

Nan, and turned . . . *that was Tom?*

All three boys were standing in the open door to the back patio looking toward their road.

"Mom! Look!"

Nan found her legs and moved . . .

If the lakefront was bad, what she was looking at was just *unbelievable*! To her relief, maybe her car had been spared. But little else! *Where was their dirt road that ran a quarter-mile out to their gate and the county road?* Instead . . . she could see only a forest of fallen trees—massive trunks of trees—huge branches everywhere! Right up to walls of the cabin.

Nan picked up the phone—

Dead. And no one in town will know about this for a long while, or even that we are out here!

She flicked a light switch,

As she suspected—dead—no electricity . . . that means . . . no pump—no water. She knew better than to try the gas stove even though it was fed by a large propane tank outside.

Glass crunched under her feet. She began sweeping.

Rob's voice came from somewhere outside:

"Mom we've got to get out of here. I'm going to see if I can find grandpa's gasoline power–saw and the extra gas cans."

Seeing Rob, and Tom struggling their way toward what was left of the tool shed, Nan called to Lyn and Vickie:

"Girls! Get some old clothes on. Find your work gloves—long sleeves! We all have to help."

"Where's Tuffy!!" Little Andy was in tears.

Nan didn't know if it was from missing Tuffy or his fright, but no one knew where the cat was. No one knew if Tuffy had been outside or in the cabin, and both girl's searching the cabin brought—"No cat . . ."

"Where is he!!" cried Andy.

Nan looked at her youngest, "I don't need another problem Andy," she told him.

But when Andy managed to slipped outside to start searching through mounds of branches Nan sent Vickie after him, *if Tuffy were lost, it will be hard on everyone. So, if possible . . .* Nan knew Tuffy had to be found, a*nd it was only—"if"—*

Pulling in a deep breath, senses spinning, Nan tried to think. Somehow she had to get them out of here. There was nothing around the lake . . . even if they could get there. The road was impassable. Going through the woods would be worse. And even if they did— they would need a car. Her car was useless. Hacking their way out was going to take time . . . *how long? But we must—*

Looking around her, seeing the cabin intact, brought some calmness, . . . *the one thing she could do immediately was make sandwiches.* She was nailing a cookie sheet over the broken kitchen window when Rob and Tom returned.

At the first sound of a gasoline power-saw, she pulled on gloves, long sleeves . . . and went outside.

The sight of young Rob tackling all those tree trunks was something she would never forget. With him wielding the saw, Tom helping, Nan and Lyn began pulling away limbs and branches. By noon a narrow path was cleared *only* to the car.

"We've got Tuffy!" Vickie was carrying a huge, trembling ball of frightened tawny fur. "He's fine, Mom. He was under the cabin."

"Poor Tuffy," Nan turned to Andy, "take him inside, and *you* stay in there with him, Andy. Someone has to tell me when the phone rings." Nan admitted to herself, *that's a bit of subterfuge.* But inside was the safest place for Andy . . .

"And I want you to *keep* them both inside," she told Vickie.

Considering . . . Vickie went around the entry patio picking up birds that hadn't made it, then sat down on the stoop with her back against the screen door.

Nan returned to watching Rob.

And when Andy fell asleep, Vicki joined Lyn and Tom pulling away pieces of trunk, limbs, huge branches! But it was Rob that Nan watched with a mingling of concern and pride. Her fifteen–year–old son was the hero, his determination becoming a lesson for all of them as the hours passed.

The tornado had struck just before eight o'clock that morning. Time moved on to three in the afternoon—to five—to almost eight that night in the summer's fading light—when the last tree blocking the road was cut up . . . pulled aside. Branches above their heads on either side. But the road lay open—not very wide—still, if she drove carefully—enough to get the car through.

Nan locked the cabin door, had everyone and the cat in the car, and drove cautiously. Turning right onto the county road. Weaving—round and round fallen trees—she got to the highway. Turned right again, . . . *said another silent prayer.* They had left much behind remaining to be done. Days, even months of work. But those would be other days . . . *She was taking her children home.*

CARRY ON

Oh Lord You came, to me one night,
Slipped into my heart,
I was unaware—
You brushed away the haunting fears,
Held me in Your arms,
Left me with a song—
So I could carry on,
Lord,
I could carry on.

Love, Laughter and Tears . . .

RACING RED RIVER
For Arnold . . .

1940's **. . . AUTO BRIDGE - RED RIVER NORTH**
Steel verses river, Ice and current,
Chilling – danger.

Photograph: State Historical Society of North Dakota

RACING RED RIVER

He heard it. Thought about rolling over . . . *go back to sleep.* Then sat up. When it came again Clint leaped to his feet—

"Sigren!"

He could smell bacon frying. 'Siggy' was getting breakfast. Grabbing his robe Clint ran to the radio flipped the switch and dialed for NEWS . . .

"Sigren!"

Why couldn't she hear him! Dancing in bare feet on the cold tile floor he hopped back and forth . . . foot-to-foot . . . until he could pull over a scatter rug. The radio sputtered and came to life just as the sound came again— *A tremendous rumbling roar!*

"Clint! Clint! Did you hear that!"

"Dad! The ice, the ice!"

All of a sudden kids and wife surrounded him, and the radio blasted on with an inane bunch of talking.

"Quiet! All of you!"

The news broadcast had already finished. Clint spun the dial again . . . *nothing but music and junk!*

Sigren took control: "Gingee, go get dressed. You'll be late for school." Grabbing for their son, she held him still until he decided to listen . . ."David, just quiet down. Go get some clothes on, it's cold. Put those pajamas in the laundry. —Right now!"

Clint spun the radio dial...

"I'll see what I can find, Clint—you go," said Sigren.

Clint patted her back and ran to get dressed—*if the ice was breaking up . . . coming north?* —He moved fast!

It came again, reverberating, shaking the floor beneath his feet . . . the booming sound of ice flows hitting together. Grabbing boots, briefcase, the roll of plans, Clint went back to the radio, sat there pulling on socks, lacing the boots.

Suddenly the radio spit out the abrupt warning he had feared:

" **. . . we are told there is no assurance the bridge will hold. Massive piles of ice are being carried . . ."**

"Sigren, I'm going! —Siggy!"

"Do you have to do this, Clint? It's crazy . . ."

"Got to get there—only way is the bridge."

"Dad—"

"Not now. I have to go. Mom will drive you to school."

"Sigren . . .?"

"I put a thermos of coffee and a couple sandwiches in the car, Clint. If you insist on this you'd better step on it."

She helped him into his jacket, gave him a kiss, and stood aside…

A thunder of pounding ice added force to her words—

That time they both felt it!

Clint put his arms around her:

"I'll be okay, Siggy. Keep warm and keep things going until I get back. I'll probably be a week."

"Call me when you get over the bridge."

"Okay, I'll call you."

"*After* the bridge, Clint."

"Okay! I'm gone—"

At least it isn't snowing... Clint pulled away from the house with the tires moving over a sheet of black ice, knowing it was too early for the sun to free the roads. He'd be careful, *that could slow him down.*

He swung onto the highway heading out of Fargo, relieved to find both lanes clear. Ahead of him was the bridge over the notorious Red River, and beyond—Minnesota. Clint stepped on the gas—

The roar of ice was deafening. There was no use listening to the radio, *wouldn't be able to hear it.* But he turned it on anyway. Then rounding the last curve before the river, what he saw made him grimace—

Ice! Piles and piles of it! Huge blocks of ice had pushed upward during the night almost as high as his house—massive ice-flows moving up–river toward the bridge, *almost as fast as he was!*

He pushed the gas pedal . . . *have to get over that bridge!* If it goes out they'll loose the job they're bidding on. He had to get through Minnesota to Duluth by 4 pm. *Must get over that bridge!* Suddenly he was praying—the bridge has to hold!

Boom . . .! Boom . . .! Ka–boom . . .!

Dynamite—! They're blowing up the ice—! Clint steadied the wheel. Kept going. Chunks of ice hit the road. Ice everywhere—

Ka–boom . . .!

They're stopping him! Highway Patrol in orange slickers . . . Pulling him over:

"Mister, we don't trust the bridge—"

"I've got to get across. More than a lot depends on it . . . can I make it do you think?

"Mister, if it was me... I wouldn't try it."

Clint looked at the long span. A small, blue truck was starting over. Several cars were almost over. He could see trucks waiting on the other side—

He looked at the river. Great pile–ups of ice, swinging and churning were heading toward the bridge. Clint guessed they would shake the span, some maybe top it. *But he thought he could make it.*

" . . . Thanks. I'm going—"

"Mister, you're crazy."

But they couldn't stop him unless the bridge really was shaking—and it wasn't—bridge looked firm . . . *looks good,* he thought. Smaller ice flows were chunked up, were passing under the center span, water churning over them . . . *but ice is moving good!*

Then swinging onto the narrow center span Clint heard the sirens. And in his rear view mirror he saw the Highway Patrol had stopped all traffic. *So he was the last one—alone except for that blue truck ahead of him—*

He looked to his right down–river and— "*Holy Might—!*"

The huge wall of ice was almost on top of him! *He couldn't see the top!* Great slabs of ice were fast bearing down on the bridge and—

He's only in the middle of the span—!

Suddenly the blue truck swerves left! . . . *Pulling up beside it he's racing side-by-side!* —Truck lays it on—spurts ahead!

He moves to follow . . . hits the gas so hard the car *jumps!* . . . *Skids! Skidding! He's Skidding!* —*Sliding* . . .*!* So Swing! *Swing!* Forcing both arms to follow the wheels straighten out straddling center . . . *and keep going! Go! Go!*

Stare straight ahead at that truck's tailgate—and keep going!

. . . *So the truck is off the bridge.*

It's just him—!

Almost there . . . glancing down, *he's pushing over 60 on a frozen iron span . . . roar of ice right beside him . . .*

Go! Go! Keep going—!

Bouncing! Bouncing off metal to road *and he's pumping . . . pumps to slow . . . pumping brake on ice*—stiff knuckles griping the wheel—slows to 55, to 40, 35, 20. . . and pulled over. *Stop!* Ahead the truck has stopped.

Sitting, Breathing hard, *he's feeling his heart jumping . . . try to deep-breathe . . .*

There's a policeman at his window:

"You okay?"

The screaming of steel and concrete is rising higher and higher drowning out all sound.

Getting out of the car, he leans against it beside the policeman watching the bridge tip—break up—a thunderous sound of booming ice and crying, screaming bridge that goes on, and on—goes on until the bridge is gone, huge chunks of steel–concrete–bridge rising up on massive mountains of ice to be carried northward as they settled.

"You were lucky, Mister . . . " *The policeman has left.*

"Shaking, Clint finds the Chevy's rear bumper, sits down. Shaking, . . . *and all of a sudden h*e's *ringing wet.*

"You okay?"

Looking up— he tried to focus . . . *this guy is highway patrol.* Clint nods, "Okay."

The patrolman moves on, Clint watching him go from truck to truck, car to car.

"Boy—man! I thought we'd had it back there!" came a voice.

Looking over at the man Clint *recognizes the cap*: "You were ahead of me in the blue truck—"

"Yea. Man–o–man! I thought we'd had it! When I saw you behind me I flew off going 60 and then some!"

"Man–o–man—!"

"Boy—man! Seeing that ice scared the hell out of me! You all right?"

"Yea . . . okay." Getting to his is feet, Clint shook his hand: "Thanks."

Man–o–man! And I got to call the wife—think those patrolmen will let us use their CBs?"

Clint came back to life in a hurry . . . *Sigren will be worried—* he stood looking back across the river at Fargo knowing it would be a long time before another bridge was in place, *he'll have to go the long-way-around to get home next week.*

"Hey, . . . you want to call? They'll call for you." The driver of the blue truck handed Clint a police receiver—

"Thanks, I'll call my wife. What's your name?"

"Luke Edwards. You?"

"Clint Randall."

"Well take care, Clint. God Bless. I've got to get a move on."

Clint watched him walk away . . . until that instant he hadn't realized the man was black. Clint watched him go, a slim man with a quick step, in a plaid mackinaw jacket and yellow cap . . .

For sure I'll never forget that cap.

He'd know Luke Edwards next time. He figured the man had saved his life.

. . . .

"Hi Sigren . . . "

"Yea . . . I'm on my way to Duluth… Yes. Okay. Just a little shaky. Made it over the bridge—last one across."

A stirring of air, belying presence,
Bringing strength to courage,
In the midst of challenge . . . **Mystery.**

IN THE WINK OF AN EYE . . .

Warm winds are blowing down in the lane,
And lilacs that winter dreary and plain,
Wear lavender clusters now that drape,
It seems to me . . . like scented grapes!
While Tulips swinging to-and-fro,
Have pushed aside the taste of snow,
Teasing hollyhocks beside my wall,
Their slivered stalks reaching ever so tall,
And roses with iris beside my walk,
Spend hours now in flower talk,
So it seems . . . *if you ask me why?*
Spring has come in the wink of an eye!

PANTS
Yea . . . !

PANTS
A neighborly neighbor,
Likes them— *Yea!*
Wears 'em all the time.

PANTS

MONDAY...

    "Wally, you've got to get rid of those pants."

"What's the matter with my pants?"

 "They're terrible!"

"They're work pants! They're supposed to look *terrible*."

"They have to go."

"Not my pants."

"You look like a tramp in those pants, they're all full of grease, paint, and I don't know what all!"

    "I like 'em, Eleanor . . . leave my pants alone."

    "Wally, get rid of them. The neighbors see you and think . . . well I don't know what they think. Just get rid of them. You look like a grease monkey."

    "Eleanor... Leave my pants alone. Okay!"

    —*Listening, Eleanor heard the door slam . . .*

TUESDAY...

    "Eleanor! Where are my work pants?"

"Gone."

"What do you mean—GONE!"

"Just gone, Wally."

"What'd you do with my pants . . .?"

"Wally, I put those stinking things in the can this morning."

"What . . .! "

    — Listening, Eleanor heard the door slam . . .

Eleanor! The garbage truck just took my pants!"

"Wally you have lots of pants. Wear something else. It doesn't matter what you wear tinkering around in the garage."

"I don't believe this, Eleanor. —My good pants!"

WEDNESDAY . . .

"Harold? Honey where *ever* did you get those pants?"

"From Wally across the street."

"From Wally?"

"Yup."

"Take them off, Harold. I'll wash them. They stink. Look terrible—all full of grease, and paint, and... Well—just let me wash them."

"I like them like this, Vivian. These are work pants."

"Harold they can stand up on their own even!"

"So? —I like them."

"Well, don't leave the yard or Pat next door will have fits laughing you off the block."

"Wally liked them, Vivian. He wore them all the time."

"Wally did? How'd you get them, Harold?"

    — Vivian knew Harold's grin . . .

"I saw Eleanor roll them up and stick them in the garbage."

"What!"

"Yup. She did."

"And you took them!"

"Right. I like these pants. Always have. 'ol Wally won't miss them . . . He has plenty. —Anyway Eleanor tossed them."

"I can't believe this."

"See for yourself, Viv. —Go ask Eleanor yourself."

"Well, put them in the machine, Harold. I'll soak them."

THURSDAY . . .

"Hey there, Harold!"

"Hey, Wally! How are things over there!"

"I see you've been pulling out those stumps, Harold. The place is sure looking good."

"Yup. Worked all yesterday and this morning. Wasn't too bad, but I've a lot of dirt to get rid of. You want some, Wally? I'll wheel it over."

"Don't need any—thanks…"

Wally stared . . . rubbing his nose . . .

"Harold, those are my pants!"

"Yup. Sure were."

"How'd you get my pants! Harold, those are my pants!"

"Pulled them out of the garbage."

"My garbage! You came across the street and pulled *my* pants out of *my* garbage can! What kind of neighbor are you anyway!"

"Oh no—"

"No? What the heck do you mean—No?"

"No."

"Where'd you get 'em, Harold? Those sure are my pants!"

"Out of *my* can."

"Yours! My pants were in *your* garbage can!"

"Yup. Figuring you don't want them… Vivian washed 'em."

"My God!"

"You mean . . . ? You want them back, Wally?"

Wally stared . . . rubbing his nose . . .
— "Eleanor will kill me."

FRIDAY . . .

"Wally, where on earth did you get those pants?"
"What's the matter with my pants?"
"Where did you get those pants!"
Wally rubbed his nose, . . . "I like 'em."
"Those—! They're your old work pants!"
"Eleanor... Leave my pants alone."
"Wally you've got to get rid of those pants!"
"I like 'em, Eleanor... Leave my pants alone."

— Listening, Eleanor waited for the door to slam! She went for the phone . . .

Love, Laughter and Tears . . .

WINTER'S FURY

All night it fell,
Snow came thickly wet, flying,
Large white flakes,
Floating, whirling down, down,
All around the wind blew,
North wind's fury,
Driving over fields,
White hiding hills,
Woods, and frosty heaven—
Seeming nowhere to alight.

BITTER BLIZZARD
Paul Bunyan's country . . .

BLIZZARD
Swirling, biting white to blind the eyes,
Or freeze the inmost soul.

BITTER BLIZZARD

All night the angry winds blew with ice and sleet. By morning a blizzard was pushing down full force out of Canada, winds sweeping over Minnesota's Arrowhead region. And one small town was getting the brunt of it. By late afternoon the winds were in a rage, forcing ice and sleet against windows of the town's Village Inn. Wind howled around corners of the low building, moved on with an unearthly shriek . . . returning twice as fierce. Gusts pinned the outside doors shut, pelting them with stinging ice crystals—beautiful—frightening, It was near impossible to pull those heavy glass doors open, and Kate was losing the struggle.

Then she saw Marj inside and waved. And with Marj pushing—as she pulled—Kate Nordahl managed to get half a leg, then her whole lightweight, 123–pound self, into the little vestibule where inner doors to the restaurant pulled easily. Marj was the only waitress on duty. She had already done the same for Jean and Lu.

Standing in the vestibule, Kate stomped ice from her snow boots and wiped the wet from her face, pulled off a knit hood and fluffed her hair. Moving inside, she walked over to hang up her heavy mackinaw by the restrooms. There it would drip, shedding ice and water into a container on the floor for that purpose.

Already Marj was at her elbow: "Coffee, Kate?"

"Yea . . . I´ll say!"

With a shrug of her shoulders, rubbing her hand together, Kate looked over at her and smiled:

"Some place this, Marj—*with 'Mosquitoes big as Moos*es *and snow to our ears!'* —So why do we live here anyhows!"

And always ready for a *Paul Bunyan,* Marj responded with her hearty laugh*:*

"Good weather for that one, Kate!"

"So . . . coffee . . .?"

"I'll have black, thanks, and strong brew. Same as those two," Kate indicated Lu and Jean with a wave of her fingers. She went over to sit between them at a front table. And when Marj brought coffee it was steaming—good, hot, and strong—*much appreciated.*

"So are we crazy or what," Kate turned to Lu, ". . . coming out in this freezing muck!"

Lu had a checkbook out, was working on figures and looked up with: "So we're crazy!"

And when Jean didn't respond, Kate glanced at her, seeing Jean lost in her own world again . . . *or she's tired.* Kate figuring it was the blizzard—wind and the dark having a way of doing that.

It had been dark since two-o'clock, and windows coated white with hoar frost made the restaurant close in like an ice cave. So it was easy to feel sleepy—like hibernating. And with every gust of wind the lights dimmed, sometimes flickered, but a soft peach glow from the light over Marj's station was making the place peaceful–sort of. *Still—*

Kate was very much aware of the wind . . . sat sipping her coffee, listening . . . *shivered.*

But it felt good sitting there. A native of the town she was use to such blizzards . . . *for sure have seen worse.* With the cold, her striking Nordic features glowed a smooth, rosy tint that made the violet of her eyes all the more vivid. Keen, penetrating eyes that Kate assured herself—didn't miss much.

Now, with all ten fingers wrapped around a mug of hot coffee she was trying to thaw out and smiled. Having been gone two weeks to the Twin Cities, it was good being here. She enjoyed these friends.

First Lu and then Jean had moved to town the previous summer. Kate appreciated their friendship. They had grown close, meeting once a week to share ideas, up-lifting each other in the never-ending struggle of living single lives, or applauding success—usually the former. The Village Inn had been her suggestion, "Only place in town that has good coffee," she'd told them . . . *and mostly we only want coffee.* At different times each had been married . . . *not something to talk about.* So now Kate sat thinking, letting the coffee warm her.

"Look! They're trying to get in!" Lu broke into her thoughts.

Two husky men were struggling with the entry doors, joined forces . . . pulled together. And one door moved. Pushing against the wind, they managed to squeeze each other through to stand panting in the vestibule before coming inside. *Suddenly* a slight, bundled–up-grey figure, emerged from the blizzard and begin a struggle with the doors, to be almost blown from its feet. Slammed against the doors full force! Turning—staggering— It disappeared into blackness...

Kate gasped! Jumping to her feet!

Suddenly a harsh shriek of laughter burst out of Lu who clapped both hands over her mouth!

Startled! Kate stared at her. Then seeing Jean still fidgeting with her pink coffee mug, Kate thought the two of them had reacted strangely. She blamed it on the blizzard.

Sitting down again, Kate *jumped* when a pounding of wind and sleet began pelting the windows. Sleet freezing to glass for an instant before sliding downward in long narrow streaks. Until blown sideways, it added to the covering of milk-white hoar frost.

Now even Marj was unnerved. And as Kate watched, Marj walked over to lower a window shade.

Glancing around the restaurant, Kate could see the two men had taken a table together, working over papers. In a side booth, an older woman had pushed back her heavy coat, but was still bundled in scarf and storm boots, working at food on her plate. She's *unnerved by the blizzard,* thought Kate, watching as the woman sat poking at something with a fork. She knew the woman was a regular at the Inn. Guessed she lived nearby, *but how she'd gotten through this blizzard, would make it home . . .* Kate couldn't imagine.

There was only one other customer. A man was sitting alone in a corner booth.

Kate hesitated—

Something about him was wrong. She didn't know what, but there was something. *Something?* She studied him, a very thin man, and tall, blond hair. Wearing jeans, he had a fur–lined jacket—thrown it back—open.

But . . . it wasn't anything like that? So what was it? Kate had a good sense of how people and things fit together—

And he was all catawampus . . . didn't fit.

Then Kate saw the boots *and was sure.* Cowboy boots with those painted "girlie" figures? And those high heels . . . worn bad. Sharp toes and cold metal, sure not for snow country, *obviously a stranger. But—*

Their small town was very-near-last before the Canada border. If the guy was traveling . . . got stuck? *No.* Somehow, in spite of a raging blizzard, he'd found the only restaurant for miles around? Off highway! Two miles into town— a*nd knew it was open! Just luck?*

He sat eating quiet like.

Puzzled . . . Kate looked around for Marj—

Suddenly he looked straight at her!

Kate turned away. Disturbed, but somehow flattered by his stare, she picked up her coffee mug—

Then from across the room Marj caught her eye, and Kate saw Marj shake her head . . .

So Marj had never seen him before.

Kate shrugged, so *that's—that.* She knew when to mind her own business and went back to sipping coffee. Still he was a puzzle. —*It bothered.*

Beside her Lu had been chuckling . . . a strange, dry sound fast turning into a wide grin.

Looking over at her Kate couldn't keep from grinning herself . . . *just had to. W*ith that wide grin, and a halo of short red hair damp and dripping around her ears, her friend could be any one of the fantastic cartoons Lu drew for a living.

Suddenly the grin went away! Lu's mouth snapped tight closed! The whole had Kate laughing:

"Oh Lu!" Kate had to hug her.

The "secret" bottle under Lu's drafting table was no secret. But she knew Lu's cartoons sold well, that Lu could afford a regular studio—not much, a room with heat and a window—but amenities Jean didn't have. *Still* . . . there were times when Lu's assumed superiority was annoying. Like that laugh . . . *That had irritated!*

Mostly Kate liked Lu. She wasn't sure if Jean did.

It was Jean who Kate had tried to help even as she had wondered why a young, and talented sculptor would come to a little town so far away from where her work could receive the attention it deserved . . .?

Then it was Lu who knew and had pulled Kate aside with: "Jean believed a guy when he offered her the world, and she followed him here. He turned out a "rotter." *And—*

Lu stung Kate with: "So I keep my mouth shut. Okay? *Wise up* Kate!"

And Kate had understood—been shocked! Frightened into silence. But it answered a lot of questions. *Still—*

She was dead certain Jean's work should be in a New York City gallery. One look at her sculptures, and Kate recognized that the girl was extremely talented. And not only skill . . . it was Jean's flair for the unusual…

"And with the right support in the right place, Jean had already been successful . . . more than successful," Kate told herself. Jean had undisputed talent—*rave reviews* from gallery shows in New York . . . Kate had seen those.

Helping herself to a doughnut Kate sat chewing . . . wondered why Jean was so quiet. *Her work maybe . . .?*

Kate offered the plate of doughnuts . . .

"No—" Jean shook her head. Morose, silent, the deep brown eyes wore a haggard look. And her fingers—

Kate watched those fingers. Jean's long, talented fingers were moving, were circling, circling on the rim of that yellow coffee mug, going . . . 'round . . . 'round, pausing only to "tat–a–tat" on her knees under the table.

Kate leaned over to her:

"How's the marble piece coming, Jean? It looked fantastic when I was over there last time. To me, it looked like you were almost finished?"

Jean stared at her—said, "Finished…"

Peering into her coffee, Jean swirled it. Coffee slopped. She made a face and took a swallow: "Damn stuff's cold!" She waved for Marj— *"Coffee!"*

Kate persisted:

"I really like it, Jean. I saw a good piece of work . . . that luster of the face is so beautifully heightened by rough places."

When Jean said nothing, Kate bit off a huge piece of doughnut and sat chewing, watching those fingers. Told herself, "The girl has it. She has real talent. Real talent,"

Kate tried again:

"It's exceptional, Jean. You have *real* talent. Somehow we have to get you to a gallery. I don't know what I can do, but I'm—"

"I . . . been too busy to get over to see this," Lu interrupted.

"You!" Jean snapped back, "You're not good enough!"

Kate looked away from Lu's pained expression thinking, *that was unkind, implying that Lu's work is mediocre.* And Kate knew it was not true. Lu's cartoon work was good. And it was income, probably more than a monthly pittance Jean must be living on after being left by some man who disappeared . . .

But Kate knew she couldn't say that. Instead— she called: "Marj!" And signaled . . . *Coffee*—

Jean grimaced, a knowing smile, "When I get to New York..."

"So . . . ?" Kate nodded.

Jean's glare turned hard, "Ya . . . and so! You haven't got it yet have you Kate? Not either of you? Well I'm not coming any more."

"What?" Kate couldn't comprehend it—

"Last time here..." Jean nodded.

Kate stiffened—felt Lu push back her chair—didn't dare look at her. That edge in Jean's voice had carried a finality Kate had not heard before. *What had she said? Had she said something?* What followed was strained silence until Marj came with coffee. Then Marj left, and suddenly—

It was Lu who leaned across the table:

"So what's the deal Jean? You tell us—'fess up."

Kate nodded, "What are you saying?"

"Deal is, I'm gone—packed up. Got a friend and saved enough. . . . if I'm careful. So I'm taking what I've got for making the New York galleries, living like I did before coming to this God-forsaken place—one-thousand, two hundred-eighty-four miles from nowhere!" Jean shook a thin fist at a whirl of wind-driven ice hitting the windows.

So . . . " Lu began...

"Yea! So!" snapped Jean,"So I've had it with backwoods . . . and you!"

"Sounds like you've *really* decided," Kate tried to stay calm.

"So! . . . Right, it's..." Jean swung—

"Are you okay Jean?" Kate interrupted. *She meant it.*

"Yeah, skin and bones," Lu's words rattled—*nasty*. "What ya' been eating?"

Kate looked from one to the other . . . *what's going on here?* Studying Jean's twitching face, seeing tears, she searched for words—

"Or haven't been eating?" whispered Kate.

"Been saving money— "

"What about all them jumpy nerves?" pressed Lu.

Kate took notice, *Lu had it right that time.* Moods and jumpiness, that's what Jean was—maybe for some time? And, thin! Kate guessed she could put two fingers around Jean's wrist! And why jittery fingers? *Decidedly there's something wrong?*

Suddenly Kate was sure. But what did she *really* know—

"This is all wrong, Jean," Kate spoke slowly, "What you're saying. It's not real is it? What is it Jean? What's this all about? Can we talk about it?" Kate put a gentle hand over Jean's fingers and shook her head. "New York is just a ploy isn't it—"

A sudden thrust! Struggling . . . Jean lurched back pushing against carpet. Grabbing for the table edge—she stood up—fell forwards— Straightened with a jerk!

Watching, Kate was all alert! Here was something she had not seen before . . . *is she ill or what?*

Lu had pulled away—Lu sat gripping a coffee mug so hard her knuckles went white—didn't move.

Looking down Kate saw the boots first. *Startled,* she looked up into the face of the *stranger* from the corner booth, her shoulders stiffened . . . Kate rose.

Faced him—

Suddenly she was looking into vacant, drowned eyes – *feeling her jaw tighten:* "Do you want something? "

"He's come for me . . ."

Jean moved—zipped her jacket. Grabbing her things, walking to the door, there was no looking back. With the stranger pushing out against bitter blizzard they were gone—

"Just like that. . . !" Kate's voice shook.

"Right—" said Lu.

"And it tells us what, Lu? You want to tell me what you know about this?"

"I know hard drugs when I see 'em, Kate. That guy's gotta be a pusher. You see his eyes? Wide, dull pupils? Them eyes were just like my brother's."

"*Brother?*"

"Jean's lover."

"Brother—your brother!" Kate's mind fought against it. "And Jean knew—!"

Lu shook her head, "Don't think, so not sure . . . so what's the diff' anyway?"

Now on her feet . . . Lu bumped into chairs with a clatter, swaying, making her way to stare out the windows for her car—

Flushed with anger Kate moved to follow. But anger left her with nothing to say . . . w*hat was there to say*? She stood looking out at a world of white— in a daze of confusion— Then her mind cleared, and she could think again . . .

Drugs! Instead of food—drugs! If only she— If she had only known! *Why didn't she?* So why didn't she see it!

Turning, she stared down at a mess of red lipstick smears on a yellow coffee mug . . . and something shook inside her . . .

Why didn't she know?

That led to another thought . . . *would it have helped?*

Motionless. Silent. Kate stood watching Lu weave her unsteady way back to their table.

Lu pulling out keys. . . . Lu signaling: "See ya—"

Lu threw a kiss and was gone.

Outside the window sleet had turned to snow. *Huge flakes, . . . beautiful soft snow coming down so thick . . .*

Even then Kate stood silent. She couldn't remember *ever* being so tired . . . or *feeling so alone*—

! LIES !

You took my hand,
And lied to me,
Then said you loved me,
And lied to me.

You stole my heart,
And left me pain,
You stole my dreams,
In lies that day.

You heard me speak,
And went your way,
Then played your game,
And lied to me.

So . . . now you say,
"I'll come again,"
But then isn't now,
My long-ago friend,
You lied my love away.

POOR BILL
So true . . . ?

DIDDLE - DIDDLE - DO

I met a tiny man,
In the woods one day,
Who said my love was untrue to me,
And I asked him to stay,
But away he ran,
Giggling a giggle with glee –
Singing – *Hey diddle diddle,*
And a diddle diddle do . . .
Untrue untrue, untrue.

I met a tiny man,
In the woods one day,
Who oh so slyly looked at me,
And I said, Good-day,
But away he ran,
Slapping his knee in glee –
Laughing – *Hey diddle diddle,*
And a diddle diddle do . . .
Untrue untrue, untrue.

I met a tiny man,
In the woods one day,
After my love had flown from me,
And he sat on a brae,
Eating onions and ham,
Then sadly wept with me –
With a – *Hey diddle diddle,*
And a diddle diddle do . . .
So true, so true, so true!

POOR BILL

"Did you know her well, Kate?"

"Know Jean? Once . . . *well* - maybe. But . . . I miss her. "

"There was something strange there," mused Bill.

He looked over at Kate. They'd been friends a long time, and having stopped on his way home, *somehow* Kate must have known he needed to talk, when she'd come out to her porch swing and invited him to sit a-while . . . *so here he was.* And Bill told himself, "No one could be more different from Jean." There's something comfortable 'bout 'ol Kate,"

. . . And now she was agreeing with him:

"You're right, Bill. I think strange was the word for Jean."

After that the two of them sat lazy-quiet for a spell, thinking how summer had gone by. Bill thinking . . . *it were always short summers in this north country—anyways,*

. . . The thought matching his mood.

And when a gust of breeze brought a sweet scent of rain, he got to his feet. Walked to the far end of the porch—stood looking out to a row of distant hills—not really seeing, or caring . . . stood trying to make some sense of things—*especially Jean.*

And Kate waited . . .

"So . . . ?" said Kate.

"I miss her too, Kate. She was sort of mixed up—wasn't she."

"But a good person," said Kate.

"Right. You know I was sweet on her, Kate."

"I often wondered."

"I was."

"You tell her?"

"She knew—" Bill shrugged,

Going back to where Kate was sitting, he moved *sort of unhurried like*—lowered himself into a worn wicker chair with a faded blue pillow that looked comfy 'okay' for sitting . . . finally said:

. . . "But you know, Kate, I never told her. Not really. Not after—"

"The grocery store thing?" Kate smiled, "I heard about it. And so that really happened?"

"It happened . . ."

Bill turned away—*noticed it was starting to rain*—looked back at Kate: "Sure did happen. Kate,"

. . . "Was obvious I meant nothing to her."

"Poor Bill," said Kate."

He thought that *a strange remark . . .!* Checked, but Kate wasn't smiling.

"Probably for the best you know, Kate. It's amazing what can happen in a grocery store…" said Bill . . .

. . . "We were at the North Side Market, and they have those little round tables . . . like with chairs so customers can get something from the deli. You know, maybe rest? Take a coke maybe—?"

"And Jean wanted a coke. So we headed for a table . . ."

· · · · ·

So's—

"Tired, footsore," Jean said. "Just a coke," she says.

And I gets her one. Then sitting there, we were alone until he comes to sit across from us . . . one table down to Jean's left.

Then—

"Mmm . . . *mm . . .!" — Jean goes.*

And I look up. *—it had been a strange sound . . .*

"Look—" Jean says.

"What?"

A poke in the ribs. *—I look.* And Jean seems amazed when I whisper:

"Uh-huh— So . . . ?" I says.

"**So!**"

I get a silent stare of disbelief. *—Want to take back my "So!" soon as I says it.* But . . .

"Look—"

Another poke! "So I'm looking . . . , I says.

And I'm thinking—

"He's good looking enough—firm jaw, mustache, tanned, even has all his hair—somewhat." . . . *Which I knows I don't.* And I tells to myself . . . *So he looks okay. A bit thin–ordinary like.* And the guy is chewing. He's eating taco corn chips, those big fat ones like triangles...

Then—I sees he's not just chewing! One chip at a time he's lifting up to eye level—carefully checks—takes a lick looking across at Jean. Places it on his tongue and . . . *he winks!*

He winks! *For some reason that angers me!*

"Mmm—*mmm . . . !"* Jean says.

"You said that, Jean," I says—*getting an evil look.* "Do you know him, Jean?"

"Maybe . . . I think... maybe I do? No... Really, I really do!"

"Jean—you don't," I says.

"Yep . . . pretty sure I do, but . . . can't think... Yep, I'm really, really sure."

"Jean—stop it!"

· · · · ·

Bill looked over at Kate,

". . . Sure I was getting a slow burn, Kate. Far as I could see the guy was a quiet sort who just wanted to sit a while—like we did. Then I got to thinking . . . *I'm better looking.* Almost said so. But didn't. Instead—

. . . *I'm chewing the hell out of my straw and sipping coke . . .*"

When—

"No ring. Not married," says Jean.

So I tells her, "Jean, I'll go over an' I'll introduce myself, then I'll tell him—*my sweet honey babe* wants to meet you."

"Don't you dare— "

"Why not?"

——SILENCE—

I'm staring at her! —d*oes she really want me to do that . . .?*

"Jean, he looks like an ordinary . . . just a person," I says— "Jean, go over yourself."

"I'd rather die."

"So die," I says, "But before you do, ask him where to get ice for a coke . . . or something . . ."

"I'll die first…"

"Jean—"

"So look at the jacket. That's not ordinary," she says.

"He's got ordinary pants, Jean . . . 'an don't look any too spiffy to me," I tells her.

"Never! I'll die first," she says. —*that's a **hot** whisper!* So I swings around:

. . . "Just ordinary, Jean," I whisper. "For gosh sakes . . . just go over and say hello. Introduce yourself or something. Ask to see that bag of chips . . . so what kind are they? Say we've noticed he really likes 'em—or something..."

"Yea, somethin'," she says.

"Jean?"

—DEAD SILENCE—

Then—

"It's easy for you," she says.

"**Me**!"

"Yea, you . . . a guy . . . it's not easy for me."

"Good Gosh, Jean—"

"Right! Look at 'im . . . classy duds, and nice face— No icky whiskers . . . *and* . . . no ring." —Jean smiles.

"So you want to meet a bum? Some guy your dog'll bit maybe . . . someone like me—a bum!"

"**Nasty**," she says.

"Sorry!" *Angry— I spit out!* "I'll go over there!"

"Don't you dare! I'll walk out!"

"Jean—"

"He's too important to bother."

"**Ugh**— Tell me another."

"Obviously important." —*she's whispering* . . .

"Obviously really important!" —*another whisper...*

"Mama Mia!" I go back to my coke, ... *lose my napkin— so go leaning down—go fishing for it ...*

"He's leaving." —*a whisper...*

"Lost your chance," I says, ... *from way under the table.*

"Maybe not..." *she says.*

—She jumps up...!

Table bangs!

—*Grabbing for the coke—sure my head–bone gets whacked !!* "Ding—Blast—It—Jean!"

"Oh Geeze, look—"

"What?"

"Just Look!"

—She plops down...!

Table bangs!

—*My head gets whacked aga*in! *I'm coming up for air ... Two sore spots!*

So rubbing my head... *I'm glaring!*

Jean is staring at me.

"So... What?" —*that's all I can muster...*

"He's leaving—"

"Sorry..." *I don't feel sorry! —why should I?*

"You don't understand, Bill."

"What!"

"G-e-e-z-e ! ! Those yellow shoes!"

. . . . .

Bill looked across at Kate, "Next thing I knowed . . . she's *sashaying—swinging–like* on those high, spindly heels . . . right after him out the door—"

He Shook his head . . . *thinking* . . . looked across at Kate:

He *tried a smile* . . . , "An' you know . . . she was right that time, Kate. I didn't understand—still don't. —Never will."

"So you got up and walked out."

"Yup…"

Bill let go *a long sigh* . . . "So's a couple weeks 'an I hear she's left town."

"Poor Bill."

"You said that Kate."

Kate nodded . . . *fighting her damndest not to grin…*

Eyes closed . . . *thinking* . . . Bill leans back *easy-like* in the comfy, old-like wicker chair . . . say*s:*

"You know, there's really somethin' *real* comfortable 'bout you— 'ol Kate."

. . . He didn't see the look she gave him.

Pulling herself up from the old porch swing Kate moved—jerks open the screen door to her kitchen. —*Stops!* —*Turned* . . . Sees *it really is raining?* Sees her kitchen—*empty?* —*Lonely.*

Kate changes her mind:

"Would you like to come in for a-cup-a coffee, Bill . . .?"

REMEMBERING

You come to me on a wandering wind,
A sound caressing memories,
So unaware of love's sweet sting,
I hear your voice in a smile of words,
See sunlight shimmer, mountains tremble,
A sound long lost to shadows fleeting,
From far and long ago.

ated with the lips — a mouth kiss.

LOVE'S REUNION

***The* . . . TWO TRACK ROAD**
Worn deep with memories,
Sounds caressing the summer wind.

Photograph: The John Noyes Downs Collection

LOVE'S REUNION

Carl heard the car before he saw it in his rearview mirror. Both hands fighting the wheel he swore—managed to stay on the road—barely, *hot words and a prayer!* Two wheels spun in loose sand where the road fell away without a shoulder—sand flying in all directions. A deserted country road was no place he wanted to end up in the ditch. The woman driving the silver-grey Porsche convertible didn't care. She flew by leaving him in a choking cloud of red dust.

He saw red—all over his windshield. Carl also saw a stream of yellow hair. That was all. When the Porsche spun back and forth ahead of him on the dirt road, *he held his breath.* Yelled out his window—

"Gull–darn, foolish woman!"

Turning into the two–track road that led to the cabin now visible through the trees, he looked for a place to park. Then he saw it. The sleek, silver Porsche had been parked in a very obvious place where it could be seen and envied. And at that instant, Carl knew *why he hated reunions.* He pulled in next to a truck that had seen better days, turned off the ignition, and sat looking toward the cabin. A crowd of people *he was supposed to know* were standing together on a patch of lawn—most likely with pointless small talk.

He opened the car door, closed it quietly, slipping to a side path where he made his way to the lakeside porch of the cabin without being noticed... *He'd take his time meeting them.*

Inside, the room was jammed.

Picking up a beer he leaned against the bar watching his former classmates. Twenty–six years. He'd only returned one other time, *couldn't think why he'd come back this time.* Was already regretting it. At that moment he was relieved that Grace had refused to come with him,

"Why should I go to that place where I don't know anyone and they could care less," she'd said.

Grace was right. But he had wanted to make the trip . . . the three hours by plane, a drive 200 miles north from Minneapolis in a Hertz rental. And he wasn't going to fool himself. *He knew perfectly well why he'd come.* Did he regret coming? *Right then—yes. He was feeling the fool.*

The beer was bitter. Putting it on a side table Carl reached for a martini, stood looking around the room and saw her—*there she is.* He'd know her anywhere. *So he'd come only to satisfy himself . . . Admit it. Okay! Why not leave?* Suddenly he was fighting himself. *This was stupid! Foolish.* He'd loved 'Shirl' once. That was over long ago. Okay! So he'd come. Okay, okay . . . so it was a dumb thing to do. Carl watched her work the crowd oozing sophistication—tall, slim and still gorgeous. She also oozed money. Someone was taking good care of Shirley Iverson.

Putting his back to the windows, he leaned against the cool glass, watched those long legs in that short dress circle the room, noticed she still had that charming way of talking with her hands. Only now, the nails were fiery red, and the bracelet sure wasn't fake. That black dress had to be expensive. *Would she recognize him?* The thought brought cold sweat.

What the devil! Carl swiped a hand across his forehead . . . *so the woman still had it. So what?* Taking his drink, picking up a fresh napkin from the bar, he made his way toward the door, *say hello to the crowd outside, get the car and get the hell out of here.*

"Carl? Is it Carl . . . Carl, is it really, really you?"

"Hello, Shirl."

"I'm surprised, Carl! Didn't know you came to these things. At least—"

"Never have."

"So—our twenty–sixth though. Figures. I guess we had to come. But isn't it the pits!"

"They've done their best."

Dark eyes, those deep eyes with those long black lashes studied him. Made him nervous. Feeling the familiar fingers on his arm, *squeezing*, didn't help. *And the eyes have gobs of mascara . . . too much goop, Shirl is trying too hard—*

"How've you been, Shirl?"

"Good. So good! Great in fact! You know, don't you, that Marv didn't work out and I've re–married—twice. They've gone the bye too. But I've done okay for myself." She looked down at the bracelet. "I'm single again, and liking it. You? —How's Gracie?"

Carl hadn't missed the diamonds—the fingers were full of them, *and her voice is full of money*. Removing her hand from his arm he reached across the bar and handed her a drink. *She'd had too many*, but the smile was wicked red. He didn't care to discuss Grace.

"We're fine. Happy. I've got three kids and I like my practice in New Orleans . . ."

"Good old Carl. Married to the ticky–tacky, itty–bitty wife and three brats—"

"You've never—"

"Forgotten? Forgotten I dumped you? Look at me, Carl. Do I look like I give a damn what or who you ever were—or now?"

"You look great, Shirley. Beautiful as ever. Are you happy? Okay? Somehow I . . . well somehow I don't think so. And I'm sorry about that."

"You're still too 'small town' for me." The red lips were fighting… It was a tight smile. "But how about getting out of here, Carl? For a drink. Just the two of us—for the old times."

Tempting? Was he tempted? He hesitated. For an instant he thought everyone in the room was looking at them. Quiet. Waiting.

Then suddenly he was okay. Carl smiled. *He'd be okay now.* No more wondering—so *he knew.* Shirley's running off with Marv was the best thing she ever did for him. *He should tell her tha*t . . . *he owed her that for the nastiness.* But he said:

"Not for sale cheap. Never will be."

It stung. —He had expected the slap. It was all he could do not to laugh. His smile was crooked, but he stood there, *stinging* . . . trying so hard not to laugh. W*hat on earth had made him say that?*

And she was gone, was crossing the room those hips swaying, back rigid, and he stood watching the crowd separate—then close in around her. *Then unbelieving,* Carl saw the long blond ponytail. *Shirley*—? Shirl had been driving the Porsche that almost ran him off the road!

He shook his head. Had turned away when that silken voice floated toward him again. Now from across the room . . .

"Is it Bruce? It is! It's really, really you? Darling Bruce, how wonderful! . . . Of course I could never forget you!"

Carl watched them leave.

Having spilled his drink, he reached for another and looked around to find someone he might know. *Anyone.* The sun had set. Lights strung around in the woods outside had come on, *No use in wasting the money . . . he might enjoy this reunion yet.* And going outside he found a seat near someone who looked vaguely familiar.

The horrific sound roared toward them through the woods. *Screams! Everyone was screaming.* Carl jumped to his feet. Making it across the lawn he found himself running with everyone else. He hadn't run like that for a long time, but he was running, and kept running, feeling as if something would burst—

Shirl! It had to be!

Reaching the dirt road he stood unsure . . . until shouts rang out of the blackness:

"There! Down there . . ."

"Why that way . . . ?"

The Porsche had crumpled to a heap of silver steaming metal against a mountain of gravel dumped beside the road for spreading—gravel rock and scattered warning lights—

Carl stared at them . . .

Orange blinking lights—blinking—blinking lights. Blood and lights—*damn blinking lights . . .*

From somewhere he heard— "She alive . . .?"

Then— "She's alive."

Carl looked down at Bruce. Had to look away—they'd played football together once.

A whisper . . .

He shook his head… Barely made it into the trees . . .

NIGHT CLOSES GENTLY

Night closes gently,
Surely the Lord walks beside you there,
Willing gentle blooms close tightly,
Against an evening's chill—
As eagles lift in majestic flight,
Across a land of haunting beauty,
Of fragile tranquility.

GALLERY
Fun with J.W...

LOVING YOU

Love is the heart's true spirit,
Promising to keep us cozy-warm,
On a cold Winter's night,
Sharing that glorious flowering,
Of Spring's enchantment,
Protecting us from Summer storms,
Love that treasures these sweet,
Golden leaves of Fall,
Having walked our days together,
Sharing life's dreams.

GALLERY

"Lizzy! Glad you're here. How's it look?"

"Jim Macafferty, you've outdone yourself!"

Liz Alpert took in the crowd of patrons and recognized several. She found a spot by his desk to stash her umbrella, then turned, shook her head at the drizzle coming down outside. The streets were rain–soaked . . . *why, oh why did it have to rain for the opening—of all days!*

She sat down to catch her breath—dug in her satchel for a mirror. Glanced over at Macafferty.

Jim Macafferty straightened a too–tight jacket over his expanse of belly, thinking he really had to exercise more. Unaware of a motion Liz knew well, he ran both his hands over what was left of his used–to–be–red hair, *knowing it wouldn't do much good.*

Looking up, he smiled. A number of patrons had gathered before one painting, "It will sell well," he told himself.

And Macafferty knew better than to move in on them. Instead, he walked over and took Liz's coat. Then sitting down beside her, he reached over to touch her hand, *kept his voice low:*

"That one will sell fast—"

She nodded. Asked, "What do you know of ESP, Jim?"

"Can't say much—"

Liz thought that strange . . . "Or an ethereal moment?"

Jim Macafferty took another swift glance around the gallery, then looked at the interesting young woman whose work was being shown with such acclaim:

"What are you talking about, Liz Alpert?"

"About possessing a gift – second sight – or call it what you like . . . seeing things before they happen, forward or backwards, and with absolute reality."

"Honest—?"

"Yes, really . . ." Liz Alpert waved a graceful hand toward one of her paintings—

Jim smiled. Whatever affected Liz Alpert he was sure he'd liked it. For some time he'd known he was in love with her. And he wondered what she'd say to that, *if he ever dared tell her?* She was so vibrant. So much younger. And he'd be lying if he didn't say he liked the money her work brought to the gallery.

"I've seldom told anyone of this," Liz whispered.

Aware . . . she smiled at a passing customer, "Thank you so much. Yes, it's a new work. Yes . . . oh thank you so much." The patron moved on. Well pleased.

Macafferty had placed his desk so he could see every painting and be unobtrusive—yet available. Liz, too, seemed content to sit for a while. He took in her shapely figure, clear grey eyes, striking cheekbones. A good artist, *and he thought she looked the part.*

He leaned over to talk without being heard:

"I'm interested, Liz Alpert. This—what'd you call it?"

"Extra-sensory-perception."

"ESP . . . Is it something that . . . should we put it in our publicity? Your brochure?" Jim waited for a response. Then when she shook her head, he ventured:

"I really know very little about you, Lizzy Alpert. Tell me—

Sensing what lay behind those words, Liz smiled. Jim Macafferty might not appeal to some women, but she'd been in love with him for ages, *somehow he always acts like he suspects nothing?*

Well, she'd play it that way if he wanted...

She also wondered if Jim Macafferty was the kind of person who would understand? Could he stay married to an artist? *But she was in for it now . . . and knew it.* Only one way to—

Liz pulled her chair closer and began:

"Well I've always had it—known what *had or will* happen—even when I was a kid. Like a silent vision of a soldier–friend killed behind lines in France during the war when his sisters believed he was still in England. And knowing that my father had gone in the ditch driving back from the Dakotas . . . said so way before the phone call came . . . spooky things like that. Scary for a kid. And when people found it hard to believe—so I stopped telling. Instead I write things down for myself, time and date. And I keep quiet."

Liz glanced over at Macafferty—

Jim nodded. She had his full attention.

"Well—" said Liz, "That's how it began. But I was in college outside Chicago, when a professor we all called J.W. pulled me aside, pressed me to begin painting in earnest. Full time. 'You need to go to the Chicago Museum of Art. Go to their Institute . . . see for yourself—' he told me.

"And I doubted? But bless him, J.W. kept at me. And I knew how he was respected for his work.
So one day I told him about a dream I'd been having for a long time, always the same kind if dream . . . a painting with draped, liquid objects in an eerie landscape. Just so strange. But really exciting,

"And well, I told J.W. and he just stared at me," Liz smiled, *remembering . . .* "

"Then J.W. said something like: 'Go to the Museum. Do self-study.*"

"So I did—the next Saturday. Then Sunday. Soon every weekend I was in those galleries, month after month . . . then one day it happened! In an instant my life changed . . . and if I close my eyes, I can re-live that instant exactly. And just like now it was raining . . . "

"So walking into the Art Institute I checked my umbrella before walking to a gallery show of 'New Paintings.' And I turned a corner... And there it was! Right in front of me! Four feet away! A painting with *liquid, draped figures and objects!* Like in my dream! But dynamic! So forceful! Painted by a Spanish artist - Salvador Dali.

"*Stunned*... I stepped back. Walked away. Turned back...

"Suddenly! Everything stopped—I was in total silence—no world around me. In an instant of stark reality I experienced an aesthetic epiphany. I was different!. I knew it! Absolute! I felt an immediate connection to painting . . . knew I would never be the same.

"And it just kept happening. Sketching in class I had a compulsion to draw our life models one-over-the-another. *Moving... alive!* Then on my first day in New York I went to the opening of the Guggenheim Museum and there was Duchamp's fantastic 'Nude Descending a Staircase'!" Duchamp became for me a kind of talisman – an artist to inspire, but also to move on in my own direction in my painting/

Liz Alpert shook her head:

"Life's so strange, Jim Macafferty.

"Good gosh, Liz, that's some story! Uncanny!"

She laughed. Looked up at him:

"You know it can happen anywhere, to anyone, at any time, Jim . . . *an ethereal moment*. It's like that instant when you first know you love someone . . . "

Liz Alpert grinned reading the look of comprehension on Jim Macafferty's face.

He stared at her. And at that moment *he did it*, Jim Macafferty kissed her.

And we will live our whole young lives,
In the joys of a living love,
You give me wings of gladness . . .
And lend my spirit song.

A TREASURE

It is a beautiful thing,
Elusive, clinging, a spell,
Enriching the soul.

It's warmth inspiring,
Spins the world glowing,
Chasing shadows.

Strong, revealing it will,
Weave its silken cobwebs,
Catching sunshine.

Yet fragile, needy,
It grows with all knowing,
Caring to care.

It's a living treasure,
Only tires for refreshing,
Seeking awareness.

Truly it is wondrous,
Existing on forever,
Poets call it love.

LOVING BRIDGET

***Woodsy*... LITTLE HOUSE**
Just for chirps and feathers,
Bringing us much joy . . .

Photograph: The John Noyes Downs Collection

LOVING BRIDGET

We children called her "That bird woman." That was so. But there was much more. It was much more than knowing Bridget cared for eight singing canaries in a little side room off her living room, or that she was the one person in the little town to whom they could take a wounded, injured bird, assured it would fly again. This was also true. And if Bridget were unusual only in this respect, it would have perhaps, been enough. But as someone implied—*there was more—so much more to Bridget.* And it was this truth that surprised her friends, that led to terrible, suspicious gossip, and finally to her denouement.

Barely five–foot–four "with the smile of an angel," Bridget Keller could be seen most days with a brown wicker basket over her arm, heading toward some needful soul. A former army nurse and born in England, Bridget had served in London during the blitz. Now in 1952 she was still a handsome, sturdy woman of quiet demeanor with kindly blue eyes, who took firm, quick steps on tiny feet shod in sturdy oxfords with square heels.

And Bridget trod the sidewalks of the town. That is, she did not drive. Instead she walked, carrying love to others in her basket . . . pulling away red–checked cloths to reveal heat pads, ointments for a massage . . . whatever was needed, and always with freshly baked buns, and good cheer. She gave generously of her skills to anyone who needed her expecting nothing in return. So Bridget made many women friends over the years. They called her their:

"Angel of Mercy."

Bridget was married to George Keller, and passing their gate made people think of English gardens and scented nasturtiums. For if Bridget stuck a seed in the dirt plot beside the Keller's walk, that seed was bound to burst into a perfusion of glossy leaves with orange, red, and peachy blossoms whose perfume drifted into neighbor's windows all summer long. That little flower garden was at a house in town. At their lake cabin blooms were everywhere. And a large, four–story birdhouse stood on a high pole attracting purple martins that fed on mosquitoes. The Keller property was the only one at their lake free of nasty bites—thanks to Bridget.

It was her many women friends who wondered:

"How can Bridget live with George . . .?"

A nurtured puzzlement that went the rounds at morning coffee klatches with:

"Is Bridget's giving so much to others a way out of her own existence?"

George's stomach, it was told, gave evidence of a man who liked to sip beer, and that humor, coarse–raw, even deadly, was offered incessantly to anyone within earshot. Although he held a good position, wore a suit every day, drove a good car—who were George's friends? He had a dog. It was a nice dog that eventually grew to look just like George. But who were George's friends?

All summer June to August, before dawn, a solitary figure could be seen through the heavy fog that lay over the lake—George Keller fishing. The soft *'put–put'* of a small horsepower engine filtering toward shore as he trolled back and forth, fishing rod dangling over one side of a sad grey skiff. And when George retired, this solitary morning fishing was an every–day–in–the–summer happening. About this time too, George's car developed a "*tick–tick–ticking*" that drove him wild. He never gave up on taking it to the town garage—driving mechanics crazy too. Never found that "*tick–tick–ticking–tic k. . . tick–tick–ticking–tick.*"

"Sweet, loving Bridget," friends lamented.

It was understood by all who received her freely given ministries that sweet, sweet Bridget never complained. That her housekeeping was impeccable. That she was an excellent, maybe even exotic cook. George had to be fed. George needed this. George wanted that. George must have clean shirts—daily—starched. Always done by Bridget, without a thought.

And every afternoon like clockwork, Bridget's firm, quick steps took her over the railroad tracks near her home . . . past the park, past a field of yellow daises, past Sam Morelli's store . . . a blue knit shawl pulled across sturdy shoulders—basket on her arm. If it rained there was a black slicker that came to the tops of rubber galoshes. In winter it was a heavy navy 'P-coat' with brass buttons, a woolen scarf tied over graying hair that curled prettily around her ears.

Bridget however, did carry something else in her basket. *Gossip.* She knew when someone was sleeping with someone else's wife . . . *or* . . . husband. She suspected the same about a neighbor—*down the block.* And when she told her friends, to their "*hot*" delight, Bridget spoke not out of gossipy malice, but in a sweet, true innocence that just accepted:

What will be—will be—

And it was about that time when a friend came to realize that those canaries, in six shiny cages in the Keller house were Bridget's children. The friend had often listened to, "Come little birdie, birdie," watching as one-bird–at–a–time flew out to rest on an offered finger. And that friend came away impressed . . . *here was love.*

Then George died suddenly in October.

And that next summer Bridget's friends found out there was more . . . so much more to Bridget. Gone was the knit blue shawl. Instead, there was a pink coat. A perky Scottish tam–o'–shanter rested on newly tinted curls. Gone were the canaries.

It was *whispered* . . . "Could Bridget have a boyfriend?"

A young man some years her younger was seen in her company. And Bridget who had always walked . . . Bridget learned to drive at the age of sixty-four! Was it freedom at last . . . ?

Bridget's "trip–trotting" had stopped.

And when the young man moved in—then didn't forked tongues *wiggle-waggle* in the little town!

Not one of Bridget's friends ever met—*nor professed wanting to meet*—the "boyfriend" who had inspired such transformation . . .

They were just . . . "*too busy.*"

In a few short months Bridget, sweet loving Bridget—all giggles and smiles had no friends . . .

But surely she had something to live for.

Love, Laughter and Tears . . .

ONE DAY

One day in June,
When I was all alone,
I walked beside the seashore,
And sat upon a stone.
I sat beside a blue sea,
And sang a quiet song,
They were God' words,
But I sang along.

CAPTAIN ANTON BERNTSEN
Of Vikings born . . .

***1800's* . . . THE BRIG**
And my road leads me seawards,
To the white dipping sails . . .

Etching: by ship artist, Gordon Grant – Dover Publications.
Reported events, in this account can only be told as fiction,
Herman Melville 1819–1891 – one source for sailing lore -
loved, and lived the sea's dangers, as did Anton Berntsen,
my Great-grandfather. — LIZZY.

CAPTAIN ANTON BERNTSEN

What was he thinking of, Anton Berntsen, My Captain? It was April 1886, three hours out of Christiania (*Oslo*), past Denmark's near point we were—in North waters 'tween Normandy and England, with open sea beyond the bowsprit (prow) of our ship's great masthead—and still My Captain had not left deck. This unlike some captains I've sailed with. Many be secluding selves three days or more after passing land of the Danes.

Not so this Captain. He being in full sight, full uniform, on after-deck noting landmarks with compass card . . . listening to the "hum" of wind in her sails, a sound like music to the ear—him being fully trusting of *me* to command.

"All yours, Mister Olavssen!"

Those were his words. And I went about my duties, being First Mate–Second-in-Command.

And I remember asking myself . . ."What are you thinking of, My Captain Berntsen? You who stand marking rhythmic swings of ship and mast, studying land and water, scenting salt–born–wind in her billowing canvas?" —*That I did ask myself.*

We would in a few hours leave coast behind. Set sails to fresh wind and turn south in our passage for rounding Cape Good Hope. Then we be on to China.

I had sailed twice before as First Mate with Captain Berntsen, over four years — it being two years to China and return. I knew his ways of command. His always pushing up my self-confidence. But never had he shared *inner thoughts*, him being a solitary man with springy step, serene brow, and being firm and fair. Him trusting his officers . . . which of course, never displeased.

I had seen his *ektefelle* (spouse), she a daughter of the Gulliksen family of Christiania. "My Gunild," the Captain said, her name slipping with a smile from his lips—Gunild Jorgine Gulliksen. And a comely look she had standing on the *kai* (wharf), those violet–blue eyes watching the fitting–out of ship. And I be told she has born him six children, Gunild who stood there with one wee lad in her arms, a son and three daughters beside her. One I guessed being Hilda Kristina of fourteen year. For My Captain's eldest, a daughter wedded, had left for America but a month ago it was . . . *I know.* For talk of that one's wedding had gone the rounds of respectful seamen on the *kai.* So there be no tearful goodbye for Gunild Gulliksen. That's a true sailor's *ektefelle* (spouse), She having at most, only ten winters with the Captain out of twenty years married . . . him being at sea.

So it's no young Captain I served. Three months short of forty–four year, he being one of Norway's respected. —Now I think how fine it was to see him up there, head thrown back, dark beard bristling, a tall, keen–sighted man in love with the sea. *Seeming to be Viking–born,* it be said of such as he. A man knowing the sea—its temperaments, fickleness, . . . *better than any I ever sailed with.*

And that April it was full sail to China again we were, and much laden with cargo, our bowsprit lifting, sails swelling, braced yards with billowing canvas, and rigging dark against clear sky . . . shimmery water astern. So it was . . . *Good–by Christiania! In two year's time we see home again!*

And with experienced crew, at sail through days, weeks and months of good seas. with fair to good weather, the passage had promise for one of the best trips, . . . *in my sea experience.*

For every seaman Christiania to Bergen jumps to be one of a crew under such a man as is Captain Anton Berntsen. That meaning—it needed only those few days sailing fjord and past the Danes, for my men to shake down into duty—find places—for routine to set. In all, only five of a twenty-man crew were new aboard on departure from Christiania that April 1886. All Norwegian seamen, and without doubt, the best in the world they be.

In truth, it makes my tale all the harder to tell—

Weeks and months fell away. Until fitted again with cargo, we be returning late May 1887, and with mementos . . . treasure for dear ones at home, carved jade, coats, Chinese porcelain of fine color and decoration, such being much wanted by My Captain. So it was those China seas that lay behind us, and we be Norway bound, all faces turned toward home with untroubled minds. It was running with full sails and favored winds purring a deep "hum" in the ropes, spars creaking. And there be singing in the air with main top-sail and gallant bending, spilling wind, to fill again when the gust passes, sails catching the faintest breeze of India's Seas.

And by September the coast of Africa be ours.

Come October it was in good weather, on Noon Watch . . . all crew being on deck . . . all uneasy before sky and sea as we be nearing, 34°21'29"–South by 18°28'19"–East, soon to be rounding Great Cape of Good Hope. That being the most southern of Africa's land . . . and to every sailor's mind it be told . . .

A wicked place, a place of witch–driven winds . . . of sea demons to swallow a ship whole—so evil be the storms!

Here with cap pulled low, standing sturdy, reassuring, it was always Captain Berntsen there beside the wheelman. Day through night My Captain stood, watching for fog off bay-or-sea, fog covered land . . .

Fog haunted by *damned, ghostly seamen - those doomed forever to the sea . . .*

It weren't fog that alerted me. But a high–pitched *"whistling"* there from the rigging—sails fast filling with a hollow *"boom!"*

And the rush of great wind—

"Shorten sails!"

Captain Berntsen ordered all men aloft. Minutes more that voice rang out—

"Get those sheets hoisted!"

Men took to ratlines and rope ladders, climbing aloft on the run, rigging soon alive with able men struggling might and main, hands enough to reduce sail, to secure stubborn, billowing, thundering canvas! Men soon be *tying themselves* secure with ropes as rushing wind began swinging wildly——driving winds bringing great thundering seas upon us from the south—then whipping full furry from land.

It was great sprays of foam off black rocks, the ship lifting in foaming, broiling sea—a straining, pounding of ship. *My feeling her shudder.* A full mainsheets be flapping—be flapping so hard, a good many men it took—flinging selves on canvas to bind it.

Then under main topsail, running fore-and-aft spankers, with My Captain at the wheel, we be holding our own . . . *so I thought.* Holding our own, and with Africa land in sight to starboard.

. . . Be holding our own when sun disappeared.

Fierce wind tore at us from all directions. Winds sounding with eerie howling turning to haunting roar! *And I heard myself hollar:*

"Orkan! Orkan!" - (*Hurricane!*)

Sheet upon sheets of deadly rain moved over us. Land and sea disappearing as a full–blown *Orka*n hit us!

Holding to our center mast I looked to the rigging, to men skidding down lines as we pitched and yawed, men swinging, bodies hanging out defiant above a maddened sea, then be climbing back—struggling, fighting upward to a determined hanging–on in the sails—tying self to masts.

And when rope parrels holding yard to mast gave way—ropes lashing! At such a time. . . . *I knew it be every man alone up there . . .*

"Min Gud—! Holdfast Olavssen—!"

My Captain's oath cut to me in a wet, howling mass of noise.

I turned—*Froze!*

A wall of black water there was! That wall rising up before our masthead! *Would she take it?*

Standing astride a thick coil of sea rope I dropped flinging the heavy rope around my waist, so roping myself to the ship's great masts. *And in a burst of unknown strength* I pulled the solid mass of ropes a-top me and lay under, be hugging ship's planking, arms in death-grip 'round the mast—

There I be holding on!

"Holdfast Olavssen . . . !" My Captain's voice went past me. In a sudden flash of light I see him—

Captain Berntsen, legs apart, holding steady—firm to the great wheel having lashed it to post—and so himself . . .

Beard dripping. Hands on wheel. Fierce eyes were staring at what was coming at us. *—Mighty Viking!*

The thought pierced my soul. My last thought that be—

With terrifying roar it took us. *Hearing ship cry out a great cracking shudder! Hearing screams!*

Underwater came sudden. Fearsome. Freezing black silence. Rising up gasping . . . panting. Fighting water! Spitting in panic! Needing air to breath! Stunned . . . battered, I be floating bound-tight to mass of planks, ropes, splintered mast, be struggling to hold with mast and wood. *—Unable to do more.*

Drifting, floating wave-tossed in black-cold sea, cold as ice—*Min Gud, how to last!*

Whatever kind of demon storm hit us—it was no more. Lifting my head . . . *only foam and rocks.* But for sure, I had seen land . . .?

There be land none. No sign of ship. I know there is no ship nor men, no masts, rigging, timbers—only water.

And *so . . . to pray is all I can do—* "So be holding to the wood," I tell myself, "Pray to be seen."

Cold, numb, how long drifting? I woud'na known when hearing shouts with hands clutching, working away ropes. Arms be pulling me bruised, half–froze, into a dory rowed landward. It was African fisher-folk saved and healed me. And weeks walking an African shore—searching . . . *searching for any sign of our ship . . .?*

Nothing. *Orkan* took everything, all souls lost. And me with only my papers in sealskin pouch, worn with neck thong next to my skin, and with naught but a small piece of ship's plank with frayed rope—it to show for surviving.

Past months to heal, year more with waiting, praying for ship with Norwegian Captain—or other willing to board me, my needing to work below with now a limp to my walking. Then being boarded for Denmark. And I hoped—Christiania . . .

. . . but now with great and fearful dread. Sore frightened! Had word gone before me? Would I be believed? Me a seaman? There was no one left to warn. None to say what might be waiting for me?

But in my mind lay the Captain's good *ektefelle* (spouse) and children. Only I could tell them *of him . . .* of *My Captain. He being courageous, the best and last I would ever sail with.*

It was with this and more passing through the mind that I sought the house I should go to from others on the kai. Then set off best I could. Even before be turning in myself with papers—

The day was warm full sun, high wind-moving clouds, the rough, worn paving stones a harsh sound under old sea boots after a ship's deck. But I had not far to go finding Captain Berntsen's house close to ship and fjord . . . *this no surprise to me.*

Then fate it be . . .

When turning one last corner I look to see My Captain's Gunild Jorgine in the narrow cobble street . . . her Hilda Kristina in the doorway. And seeing me, Gunild knew—*seemingly expected me*, her Captain then 'most two year overdue.

Nervous, I spoke quietly what I knew, giving wood bit and rope to those gentle hands . . . a*ll I could offer.* Then sitting a time, offered *lefsa and sweets* I be not able to refuse, in time I left to face my own fate.

It was some time after when it be told My Captain's second daughter, she Hilda Kristina now of sixteen years, would sail for America. And I wish her well that daughter of My Captain.

. . . . . .

. . . Here then are words I promised when beginning this, my telling of Captain Anton Berntsen of Christiania. I pray he's resting at peace My Captain, in the sea he was born to and loved,
— *First Mate, Olav Olavssen.*
(True name yet unknown.)

Norway law 1800's : A wait of years to legalize / affirm death at sea.

Norway Parish records affirm :

>January 1893, the Marriage of :
>
>"Gunild Jorgine Gulliksen – to – Thorvald Torgersen.
>
>He being a seaman younger than herself. "

—MARRIED—

January 1893 - Eau Clare, Wisconsin
Hilda Kristina Berntsen, 23 - Born Oslo, Norway.
Hans Hansen, 26 - Born Lillistrome, Norway.
Founders of their American family:
Four daughters, five sons.

Love, Laughter and Tears . . .

ON MAIN STREET

It was always special on Main Street
Twelve blocks away at the center of town,
Where parades were held,
And trains came in from places unknown,
At a depot Grandpa built,
From Main Street loved one's went to war,
To Main Street most returned,
While we were left with
Flanders' Fields,
Their - "Poppies row on row."

From Main Street they marched off to war,
First Erv and George, Rod, Bob and Carl,
Then Will and Dick, Jim and someone's Beth,
While golden stars spread through the town,
For those who didn't return.
And tears were shed on Main Street,
There, in my hometown.

From East to West on Main Street,
As school bands played,
And scout troops marched,
Came Veterans swinging all in step,
Marching, marching, with *Old Glory*,
Marching 'round the curve,
In every parade on Main Street.

It was always special on Main Street,
The center of my hometown,
With wars - in seven out of eighty-seven
Or every eleven years,
And tears for a lifetime through.

THE ELEPHANT'S TRUNK
Vilee remembers...

Dainty little violets
Smile and nod endearingly,
Charming all they meet.

THE ELEPHANT'S TRUNK

It was 1919 and now it was August, Violet thinking 1919 a nice number. And she liked this time of summer when the mosquitoes were not so bad, there was not as much rain—not like last night, But still a little. And she knew it could be warm for two more months. Besides—she had turned sixteen in April. Violet smiled thinking about that too . . . sixteen was "grown-up." In two weeks she would be in high school. Yes, she liked the number 1919. Kept saying it like music as she walked. Momma Kristina was sending her to the store for thread and buttons, and twelve whole blocks . . . an hour away from Momma! Violet relished her freedom.

Then pulling her sweater closer, she reminded herself that Momma was waiting, so she'd better go faster. "Hustle Violet," Momma had said. And when Momma said something like that . . . everyone moved—*fast!* Violet stomped a puddle! Stomped again and had to shake her shoe dry.

She was always the one to be sent, *sure, because there was no one else to send!* Florence was at teacher's college in Bemidji. Gertrude, or Dotty? Violet knew Momma would never send them! Gert was sort of loopy at thirteen, and Dotty, who Momma called "Doka" . . . , well Dot might not come home for hours. Bob had just started walking better after polio. And Willard, who Papa Hans now calls "Petey", her sweet little brother was only six. *So* . . . she, Violet, was always the one to be sent.

That puddle had been too deep! She had to stop, shake out both shoes, then wipe them. And telling herself, again . . ."Of course there was no one else to send," Violet brushed away a sudden tear. She missed her brothers. Erven, her wonderful Erven with his funny jokes and *crinkly*, laughing eyes—Erven had been badly hurt in Germany fighting the Germans with George—fighting Germans in the World War, both her older brothers. George was the tallest and kind, quiet, so like papa Hans—*but Erven*—

Violet guessed maybe Erv would be her favorite . . .

Erven was the one who started all of them calling her "Vi'lee," when she'd told him how much she hated her name.

"Momma gave nice names to all the rest of you—But no! I have to be Violet Hazel!"

—Oh how she hated it!

"I'm absolutely not *a prissy* flower," she'd told Erv. So he'd started calling her Vi'lee. And somehow it fit.

George was coming home, but Erven was in that New York hospital, and it was Erven she missed the most. And she guessed he was the smartest of all of them, even if he liked to play jokes—like sitting on Momma's lemon pie! Violet was *sure* he'd known the pie was cooling on the chair—Momma always put her pies there. And when Momma chased after him with a board from the pile . . . did he ever run! The memory of it left Violet laughing aloud in the middle of the sidewalk.

Embarrassed, she looked around quickly. But saw no one. Both street and sidewalk were deserted. *And muddy!* She would pick her way carefully after that last puddle. The sidewalk was new since fire had burned the town two times. That was before they moved here, but some of the streets near her house are paved with tar-blocks and smelling of sweet creosote in the summer. —She liked that.

Getting to Main Street, Violet turned into Woolworth-Five-and-Dime. Then surprised and pleased, finding that Momma had given had given her an extra nickel to spend, she emerged with a triple-scoop, strawberry, vanilla, chocolate, ice cream cone in one hand, the bag of thread and buttons in her pocket . . .

And that was when she made a fateful decision.

She turned east on purpose, walking along busy Main Street toward Third Avenue. Leaving home she had walked twelve blocks of Fifth Avenue on her way north to the center of town. Now she would walk home by going south on Third Avenue.

"And for good reason—" Violet assured herself.

On the corner of Third Avenue South and Second Street, stood the high school she would be going to in September. Only two weeks! She had never bothered to look at the old school . . . now she was going to.

And looking at it—

"Ugly!" She whispered, "just plain ugly!"

She did not like ugly things, not ugly colors, frogs, boys or turtles, not anything ugly—especially not brown things—*and that is ugly brown!* How was she ever going to last going here! She had seen the new high school with its tall, white pillars that was being built on Fifth Avenue, and knew it would not be finished until Spring . . . *So?*

"So I must go here!" she whispered.

". . . It's just plain ugly!"

Violet stared at the old, brown wood building. Large and square, it stood a high three stories. She walked to the front entrance where a sign said: VIRGINIA HIGH SCHOOL. Looking up, Violet saw there were not many windows, and supposed that was because of their winters? *So she just knew it would be dark inside—didn't like that either.*

"Ugly!" She told herself. Finally said it *really loud*:

"That's just really ugly!"

"It is, isn't it . . .," said a voice.

Violet whirled, "Oh, I didn't see you!"

"I know. —But I think it's ugly too.

Looking at her, Violet didn't think she'd ever seen the girl before. In fact, Violet thought she looked *very different*. Being Norwegian, she herself was very fair, had blue eyes, was tall and thin. This girl was short and sturdy with ruddy cheeks, her hair cut short in a bob and . . . *very* brown eyes. "In fact she's pretty," thought Violet, "just different."

Suddenly she realized the girl was talking to her—

"What's that?" the girl asked again— "What's that long thing curving down to the ground—what *is* that?"

"Good heavens—I don't know," replied Violet, "what on earth *is* that?"

Violet stared at a metal "tube like thing" that was sticking out of the third floor at the back of the building. Now she could see that it ran all the way down to the ground.

"Looks to me like an elephant's trunk!" the girl smiled with a hearty chuckle . . .

"Are you going here too?" asked Violet.

"I suppose so," the girl smiled again. "I'm Myrtle Biederman. I'm new here."

"Well, I'm Vi'lee . . . Violet Hansen. I'll be in tenth grade."

"Me too," said Myrtle, "and I think I've seen you walk by my father's butcher shop . . . it's on Fifth Avenue South near Tenth Street . . . by that elementary school." She added quickly:

"But really—we don't live near there. We've just moved here—my younger sister and brother too . . . and my Father. He's from Germany."

"I live on Eleventh south . . . off Sixth Avenue," offered Violet, thinking fast—because—*from Germa*ny, made her feel a bit strange. Also she thought Myrtle sure smiled a lot! Still . . .Violet sort of liked it. And she had been trying to smile more having been asked once why Norwegians don't smile much.

"I don't know anyone here yet," said Myrtle, "I know it's going to get pretty cold."

"My parents are from Norway," said Violet, "we're used to it." And when the girl didn't seem to know what to say to that— Violet pulled out her package:

"I have to go now. Momma is waiting for this, it's thread and buttons," . . . and Violet tried to smile.

"My mother died last year," said Myrtle. "She used to call me Mi'ko," . . . then seeing Violet's reaction, "But it's all right. We're fine now—I may have a step-mother soon . . . I like her." Myrtle smiled, "I do the cooking, and I like to . . . I'd like to be a *real* chef someday."

"I'm sorry," Violet shook her head. She guessed her reaction was why Myrtle said that about being a chef . . . now she didn't know what to do? And watching Myrtle walk away Violet decided, *I like you Myrtle Biederman, something about you is very nice.*

Unlike anyone else Violet knew, Myrtle wore long black stockings and sturdy oxfords, and her skirt was a bit long. But it was the walk that impressed Violet . . . *she thought Myrtle walked straight as a pistol.* So when she found out what that 'elephant trunk' was, Violet knew she was going to find Myrtle and tell her. Maybe she would have a friend.

Violet also knew she'd better hurry or Momma Kristina would be out on the porch—looking for her with—*that look!* Being a good runner, she fairly flew.

Come September, having to walk to-and-from the high school four times a day—fourteen blocks each way—Violet decided it was *just too much!* So from the first day she would carry her lunch wrapped in a cloth bag—what ever Momma put out for her—an apple maybe, always some kind of sandwich. They were not rich, so she couldn't have some of the strange Italian or Finish goodies other girls would have for lunch. But Papa Hans, being the Estimator for the Weyerhaeuser Company's huge lumber mill, Papa carried his lunch too. Violet knew, because she was the one who put it into his lunch pail.

And she planned to wait on the avenue after school to walk home with him, *and* they could take the path beside the train tracks where the fields were so pretty with wild flowers. Her Papa liked to give her arithmetic problems to solve, and with so many brothers and sisters at home, Violet felt closest to Papa Hans.

But in getting ready for high school, and with all the work to do at home, she forgot to ask Papa Hans about that 'elephant trunk.' Her first day as a tenth grader she found out in a hurry—

A large, formidable woman, Miss McDermott stood filling the doorway to their classroom:

"Everybody line up! Get in line!"

Violet stared . . . Line up? What is this?

All tenth grade classes were on the third floor of the high school, and having run the last two blocks to the school . . . plus two flights of stairs . . . she was still catching her breath when the order came again—and louder:

"—Line up! Make one line!"

"We – are – *not* – children - anymore!!" Violet told herself—

But facing Miss McDermott, who argued! They lined up. And Violet found herself last—following—walking quickly down the long hallway to face the end wall.

"Attention!" ordered Mss McDermott.

But daring a look back, Violet saw every classroom door stood open, and with students waiting? —*What is this?*

"Stand so you can see me!" ordered Mss McDermott. And turning around, she swung open a door in the wall to—*instant silence!*

"Sometime today," said Mss McDermott, "there will be a fire drill. When the horn sounds you will get in line—walk quickly to this tube—No running!"

Violet stared at a huge black hole! Nothing else on the wall! A big black hole! Moving forward in turn, Violet peered into it—

Looked right down the 'elephant's trunk!

—And a chill ran from her toes all the way up her spine, making her give hers shoulders a shake . . .

And Miss McDermott wasn't finished:

". . . one at a time you will sit on this ledge—give a push—slide down to the ground," said Miss McDermott "Do not wait! Move quickly! Absolutely no pushing! In sliding down keep your feet out straight—hands in your lap. *Never!* Never touch sides of the tube! Outside you must move away quickly to clear the way for others behind you."

Back in the classroom Violet sat trying to think, pulling her thoughts together . . . *that black hole looked scary.* But with five brothers she felt used to scary things . . . and she was agile and skinny. But she wondered about some of the others? Still that hole did look pretty big . . . *and scary.*

Her next thought stunned—*did Florence or her brothers go down that escape tube? Why hadn't any of them told her?* —Just wait 'til I get home!

. . . . . .

"WOW! It's a horn all right!" came a shout!

! A Fire Horn Was Blasting !

Furious! Deafening! Menacing!

Violet stood. Moved to the door . . . *alright . . . I can do it . . .* Walking down the hall she stood waiting her turn—

When Suddenly—

Violet saw Myrtle. And immediately she knew—

Myrtle was panicked!

—Told to, "Get on the slide" —*Myrtle did not budge.*

! The fire horn was blasting. !

! Blasting ! ! Blasting!

—*Myrtle stood silent—could not move.*

Other students sat on the rim of the hole—others were sliding—going down . . .

—*Not Myrtle.*

! The fire horn was blasting !

—*Myrtle seemed frozen . . .*

At that instant, something told Violet what she had to do— Ignoring Miss McDermott - *pushing through the lines* - Violet smiled and took Myrtle's hand:

"Would you like to go down with me, Mi'ko," she whispered? "You can sit behind me, hold on, and we can go down together."

Myrtle nodded.

. . . . .

"So . . . that is how we did it—" said Violet, "With Myrtle's arms around me—I pushed off ! —Down we went ! !

Vi'lee and Mi'ko . . . friends for life."

YOU ARE MY FRIEND

You are my friend,
My treasure more than gold,
'Tho the miles may be far,
The years so many,
Gilded with laughter,
Washed with tears . . .
Blessed with smiles.

You are my friend,
Our fingers mingle,
'Tho miles be far,
Gilded Years be many,
Loving you brings joy,
Thoughts whispered . . .
On the wind.

You are my friend,
Dearest Bonnie friend,
A treasure more than gold,
How blessed am I.

Love, Laughter and Tears . . .

THE SIXTH *of* JUNE

***Silent* . . . WOODS AND MEADOWS**
A tangle of years,
Born away on wandering winds.

Photograph: The John Noyes Downs Collection

THE SIXTH *of* JUNE

I. June 6, 1948—

"Mercí, . . ."

Keeping his voice low, Arno took the slip of paper from the man behind the desk, replying in what he hoped was *passable* French. After a quick glance, he folded the slip, put it into his pocket. The doors slid open. He stepped out into brilliant sunshine. Tall with deeply tanned face, maturity and command rested lightly on his young shoulders. And from a hushed cluster of persons standing nearby on the platform a woman recognized the uniform of an American Naval Officer. She nodded to him. Arno returned her escort's salute.

Shading his eyes, he turned to study the scene below him seeing a vast beach that ran out of sight to his right, curving beyond eastern headlands—a hot beach—sands glistening under a relentless sun and devoid of life. Arno looked away. He focused instead on an imaginary point above the horizon—

Over there beyond the water lies England . . .

Then water and sky became one—fused to a blur. Arno closed his eyes against a hurtful brilliance. Voices passed. Quiet voices . . . hushed murmurs floating out into a surrounding stillness while he stood lost in memories . . .

. . . *Memory of a different beach,* the lake shimmering in the midst of northern woods—trees scented with the first fresh bloom of spring. That was how it was that June. He could feel it, smell it, could call it back in his head. "Five years," he whispered a feeling—*a stirring . . . he and Ted with little Eve tagging along . . .*

II. June 6, 1943—*A tangle of years born away on wandering winds.*

He remembered how the grass had been up to his belt buckle that June 1943. How it felt . . . , a prickly hot grass that stuck into him right through his old jeans. Remembered how it had dug into his flesh—how he had pushed it down with every step . . . *pushed, pushed*, and kept walking—into what . . .

They had come several miles since leaving the dirt road that would take them back to the cabin. Ahead of him an abandoned, two-rut trail was almost hidden. It ran straight eastward through the narrow meadow surrounded by patches of lacy, sun–tipped woods, while to the north a high cliff loomed over the land topped by a formidable ridge of rock and trees. Then an open field became visible through the trees ahead, and soon he was in it—a vast field of golden wheat–grass rolling in all directions under a cloudless sky. Waves and waves of grass wonderfully caressed by the wind.

He pulled in a deep breath, let it out slowly . . . *had someone cleared the land?* Or had some settler just found it like this—had tilled the soil and lived an isolated life here in the woods? Many of northern Minnesota's first pioneers had done that . . . *many still did.* The thought brought a whisper…

"*There is majesty in woodland that enters into the soul . . .*"

Arno couldn't remember all the words. Didn't need to. It was enough the poet had put into words what he, himself, felt so keenly—
"*A person could find some real peace with his thoughts making his way through woods and meadows, all earthy troubles sloughing off to blow away . . .*"

He let the words slip off his tongue. *Some day* maybe he would be a writer and pen words like that.

The breeze went its way too soon. It was growing warm. To his left, the bare face of that high cliff was an enviable cool mass of glacial rock, its rugged face glowing purple-red and lavender with the sun on it, seeming like cliffs of Laurentian Mountains to the north.

Even trees on that high ridge topping the cliff look dark and cool . . . Arno twisted to look up at the ridge. Great, tall trees . . . Norway pine? *No.*

No, he decided . . . *Giant blue spruce.*

Trees that huge had to be blue spruce, and at the edge of a forest stretching far off to the north. Staring up at them Arno was sure. He felt a sudden twinge of *uneasiness. Ageless . . . silent trees—*like woods always seem to be—*until you walk in them!* And somehow those huge trees seemed to pass judgment . . . stood rooted like sentinels watching the three of them move across the land— ?

Arno shook it off. Stopped to pull off his jacket. Tied the arms —slung it to his back.

Yet . . . once that uneasiness crept into his consciousness, the feeling stuck. Given the distance, the rising warmth, his struggling over the ruts, *and his anger with Ted*—he guessed it was hardly surprising that remoteness and solitude had begun to work on him.

There wasn't any noise, just his older brother's whistling as Ted paced on ahead. *That was a funny sound,* it was as if Ted were pulling his breath in-and-out through a water reed—not a real whistle. Soon, even that stopped. It was so quiet even a whistle seemed out of place. Arno looked long and slow over the field.

Arno was irritated, *even worse—he was for sure—frustrated!* He had expected to tell Ted his news. Had been ignored. And now doing this! Maybe—*probably* . . . there was nothing left of the old farm. Now disappointment heightened his uneasiness, added to his frustration, as he watched Ted getting too far ahead of him—

The night before, even with Ted's graduation from Med School being only days away, Ted had surprised the family by driving the 300 miles north, and seeing his brother drive up to the cabin, he had been delighted! Since his own graduation from Junior College the week before Arno had been eager to share his own news, *sobering, important news* . . . only to have Ted push by him in no mood to listen. Instead Ted had gone into town to see Sally.

Having wrestled with his feelings all night, Arno knew he'd felt better at breakfast. Had agreed when Ted wanted to explore the old farm. *But this was all wrong! The whole morning!* Arno felt his anger rising. *Everything!* His brother was not about to talk . . . let alone listen. —*He's in a real funk!* So how to break into that sour mood? What was bothering Ted anyway? *Something*— Arno couldn't figure, but it was obvious.

Listening to the swish-swish of their footsteps the *silence* had begun to bother. That included those trees staring down from that high ridge. Arno began to wish they didn't have their little sister along—

"My Gosh! He'd forgotten Eve!"

He swung around! Was she still with them—Eve? She was . . . and with the bottom of her jeans rolled tight, socks pulled over them to ward off the bees coming out of that clover. *Smart kid!* Seeing that Arno felt better. Grass was up to her waist, but as he watched, Eve was coming along all right.

Turning back he could still see Ted ahead of him. But now their kid-sister was also a worry.

It was Ted who'd argued . . ."Let her come along." Now he was ignoring her . . . *Ted ignoring both of them.*

Arno frowned. So it was up to him to keep an eye on Eve—a nuisance! She didn't belong out here.

Course, neither did they—*did they? But maybe the land doesn't belong to anybody, . . .* he hoped . . .

"Last thing we need is for some old geezer to come out from behind a hill with a shotgun an' catch us on his property, and her behind to worry about!" Arno flung out the words to anyone who would listen. No one did.

He turned around again—

"Come on Sis . . . catch up. Speed up!"

Arno didn't hear what she said, but she'd said something. Suddenly he had to admire her guts—

"Come on Sis!"

"Go on!" Her voice came back at him—angry that time: "I'm fine . . . legs not long as yours!"

Ahead of him, Ted was shouting something. It sounded like:

"Why'd she want to come along for? Only twelve years old for Pete's sale! Mom should've kept her. Who knows what's around out here . . .?"

Arno stared at his back, *couldn't help himself*—snapped back:

"Yea, but a pretty feisty twelve! And it was *you* said *okay!* Don't worry about Eve. I'll keep my eye on her."

"You'd better!"

Arno had to think about that a while . . .

What the devil was eating the man? Something was definitely chewing him. And it wasn't anger either. *Worry?* What the heck did his brother have to worry about—neat internship waiting for him—good hospital...

Now . . . slowing down to help Eve catch up, suddenly Arno realized Ted was out of sight . . . *Dang! Why's he so unreasonable?*

"Hurry up Sis . . . got to catch Ted!"

"Don't worry about me. I like this."

Going over a rise Arno couldn't see her anymore . . . couldn't see his brother either. Suddenly finding himself alone, he ran to catch up to Ted:

"Hold up! Better wait for Eve!"

But Ted had already stopped. And when Arno got to him, his brother was looking out across the fields at a pile of rusted metal.

"Reaper's over there—" Ted pointed.

"You've been here before?" *Why the devil hadn't he said so?*

"Once with Sally. We didn't go far," said Ted . . . soft, quiet words. "Think that house you saw from the trail is really up here Arno?"

"Maybe . . . Maybe down that slope ahead."

"Maybe—" said Ted.

"Hey, you, guys!" Eve's giggle caught up with them.

Arno poked Ted, "She laughs at everything." Sometimes Arno found it annoying—*right then it wasn't funny.*

Putting out a protective arm Ted walked Eve into the field to where a pile of reddish, rusting iron was all that was left of a reaper.

Eve's kick was well aimed— Clang! The seat tumbled down — a 'ringing' clatter!

"*Awk!*" . . . "*Awk!*" . . . the grouse rose on its tail with a great squawking and beating of wings! Scuttling along . . . it took off—

Pretending—Eve swung . . ."ka-POW! POW!"

Ted stared . . . "Arno—?"

Arno shrugged, "So Dad's been teaching her . . ."

A pull on a hair-braid— *A push*— And Ted laughed: "Good shot, kid!" That was all it took for Eve to grab him around the waist, beginning their tussle . . .

And watching the two of them Arno had to grin knowing Eve had a way about her—and if anyone could cheer up their brother he figured Eve might. Arno turned back to the old machine. A pair of long metal arms for hitching horses lay at his feet. All grown over . . . *Abandoned? Rust–eaten clean through.* A huge machine just lying there a-heap . . . it puzzled him—

The whole place was a puzzle. Arno's sense of something wrong shifted, *from suspicion to certainty.* It's just wrong . . . good land abandoned, and fast, *real fast!* Why would that be? *For sure it puzzled—*

"Probably too big to put in a barn—"

Ted's voice . . . Arno turned, relieved to see Ted smiling.

"Is there a barn?" Eve's words came out a whisper . . .

Arno could see she was beginning to feel spooked— "Must of been that grouse breaking the silence," he told himself. He also knew that anyone hearing that grouse would know they were trespassing.

Arno told her to stay close.

"Well, it has to be down that slope ahead if there is a barn—or was one," said Ted, "This reaper had to be pulled by horses, and in our cold country horses need a barn."

"Ever wonder why they just up and fled?" whispered Arno.

Ted didn't answer.

So he doesn't know either, Arno decided.

Suddenly Eve was no longer with them.

"Hey!" Ted's heavy voice broke the silence—went thundering across the meadow, "Eve!... Where're you..."

"Look here!" shouted Eve. "There's a wheel... and another!"

"... Another huge wagon," mused Arno running his hand over the wheels. And looking at the hay wagon's heavy planks... they were silvered from snows, years of summer sun and rains. The wagon's center had caved inward, but the iron wheels were strangely upright? Then not too far away Arno saw remains of another machine. He decided... maybe some kind of plough with that long bar of blades? Turning. Puzzled? He stood looking across the deserted fields *... a reaper? Large hay wagon, and now this. Why? What else?*

It came to him then—the reality of something happening to a large family. *Had to be!* The farmer's wife would have helped... children? Sons—many sons! *So what happened here?* Fire? Murder? Arno's uneasiness, *went up another notch*. Listening, he heard only crows, bees in the clover, crickets buzzing—nothing else. *What did he expect to hear? To find?*

Looking up at the high ridge? *Nothing... no one.* Arno swallowed. *Suddenly they were miles from nowhere—*

"I'm going on ahead," said Ted.

For a moment Arno hesitated, stood watching Ted go before he took off on a run to catch up.

"Me too!"... Eve's cry, "Don't leave me behind!"

Moving down-slope, razor sharp wheat-grass was even longer, and Arno pushed it away with his elbows to spare his hands. Finally he had Eve hold on to his belt behind, keeping her close, as his thoughts flicked from—black bear—to his rifle—to having left even his pistol back at the cabin. *How stupid not to even have his pistol! What was he thinking!*

Ahead of him Ted's jacket flapped open.

Arno saw the holster, . . . *so Ted is packing it.* That helped, *but he was still disgusted with himself.* He knew the woods too well to have done something so dumb as to come away without any protection . . .

He looked back, . . . *what if Eve scared easily?*

"Eve—hold on. Stay close . . ."

"Bet they lost their water," Ted's words floated back.

"Maybe they all died," whispered Eve.

That made Arno's skin creep! This was not about water—not such abandoning of expensive machines, *something happened here. Murder? Animals?* Thoughts assailed from all directions. Just as fast Arno discarded them . . .

Telling Eve to, "Just keep up," he dug his heels into the ground—sliding—half-running down the steep slope fighting to keep his balance.

Then Arno saw it —

Ted had stopped. Moving up to him, Arno warned Eve, motioned . . . '*quiet* ' . . . pointed to the house.

Something sent out a barren, ghostly feeling making them wait in silence. No one moved. Old, gray-weary the small farmhouse stared back - dead silent.

It stood in the midst of spent, brown wheat-grass pressing up against plank walls. Dark woods behind. No barn. Above their heads one small window stared out at the high ridge. No glass. Seeing pieces if wood on the ground, Arno knew how the window had been covered.

A large slab of granite rock was dug into the ground for a step—and above it . . . where a door should have been—

Seeing that *large hole of gaping blackness*, Arno pulled in a sharp breath and with it came flooding *that strange feeling—a sense of something Arno could not comprehend . . .*

"*Empty,*" came Eve'*s* whisper . . .

In that instant Arno knew! He knew why he'd been so uneasy — *Emptiness, a chilling aura of* "*dead emptiness*" . . . *as if all life had fled . . . never existed. Even the silence seemed wrong!*

He stared at the house . . .

"Not where you'd want to come alone," Ted whispered

"Yeah. That's what I'm thinking,"

A soft *"click—" Hearing it*—at the sound—Arno looked over at Ted? He had opened his holster . . . took the clip from his pocket, slipped it into the pistol. Their eyes met . . . Ted motioned—

Arno ignored the tenseness that gripped him. More than ever, he didn't want their sister here. . . motioned to Eve . . . '*wait here.*' To his relief she agreed—sat down.

Pistol drawn—Ted began to move. Bent over away from the window, he crept down-slope, flattening himself against the wall and sliding along it, waiting beside the hole's gaping blackness.

Picking up a good size rock, Arno circled around to the other side—pressed tight against the wall. *Listened? —Heard a strange flapping sound. Soft crackling?* —He motioned . . .

Ted nodded. He'd heard it too.

Crouched to spring, Ted peered into blackness. Looking over at Arno he raised '3' fingers—disappeared into blackness . . .

1-2-3 minutes. . . one foot on the step—Arno was inside. Dropped to one knee—*so wait . . . let the eyes adjust—*

Ted?

Footsteps. Ted? . . . from the back room—

"Nothing," said Ted. "Empty. Two rooms. One window."

"Strange . . . that flapping sound has stopped," said Arno.

The old house didn't offer anything except animal droppings, feathers and bones where animals had dragged their kill inside. He had to admit it didn't look like anyone was taking refuge in the place.

Puzzled? Alert—Arno joined Ted at the window where that high ridge appeared to him as *almost protective* looming over the little house as it did. Both cliff and trees would form a barrier to hold back snow, fierce winter storms from the north. . . . *Protective?*

"A stove was here," Ted pointed to a hole in the wall.

"Like our wood-stove," came an awed voice, then a giggle—

"Eve!"

"Well I didn't like it out there by myself," she said in answer to the looks they fired at her.

And turning her back on them, Eve walked to a far wall, stood a moment . . . called out:

"Newspapers. Why newspapers?"

Arno walked over—

Every wall was covered with thick layers of newspaper, sheet upon sheet of old newspapers, yellow-brown sheets cracking–crisp with age. Some were hanging out into the room . . . and as Arno watched, they swung back and forth in a fresh breeze from the door. He'd found the flapping sound.

Eve looked at him, "Why newspapers?"

"For warmth," said Arno. "But with forty-below winters it's beyond me how anyone ever survived here with only a stove."

Ted spoke from the window:

"Determined, Arno . . . determined and strong willed. That *hardy pioneer spirit.*"

"Strong, brave too," reflected Arno. "Had to be. But why . . ."

"Hey!" Eve's shout interrupted. "Hey Arno, look at this paper! Wow! War 1918! And someone circled it with black?"

Ted whirled around, "World War One!"

"That's it!" Grabbing it, Arno read the headline aloud:

! WAR DECLARED !

"Ted! That explains it—what happened here! Sons that went to that hell of a trench war—fought in those murderous trenches . . . *and never came back?* Maybe *all* of them! Maybe even the *father here—*"

Arno froze. Something had gone wrong with Ted's face. *Suddenly everything fell into focus.*

"Brother?"

Ted nodded, "Pearl Harbor has changed everything Arno. I've got my orders— I'll report in two weeks—Marines. Have to tell the folks tonight . . ." he pulled a deep breath. "And Sally . . . Sally wants to get married tomorrow. Somehow she's got the license."

"Ted—"

Arno hadn't planned to tell it this way. *Not like this—it just happened . . .* Arno held out his hand:

"Ted . . . I'm Navy. I've enlisted."

III. June 6, 1943 – June 6, 1948.

—Five years born away . . . over there lies England.

Arno blinked . . . pulling himself from then - to now... Stood looking down at a beach where hot sands glistened under relentless sun. Quiet voices passed . . . hushed murmurs floating out into a surrounding stillness.

Arno stiffened. In one smooth motion he raised his hand in a slow, silent salute—

June 6, 1944—Omaha beach . . .
D–Day on the bloodied sands of Omaha beach.

Winston Churchill, to House of Commons: *June 6, 1944:*
"*Omaha beach . . . enemy fire and mine fields . . . scaling of bluffs undefended . . . the coast of France . . . landings on the beaches are proceeding*" . . .

Franklin Delano Roosevelt, radio message to the American People:
"*Almighty God: our sons, pride of our nation, this day have set upon a mighty endeavor to set free a suffering humanity. The darkness will be rent by noise and flame. Men's souls will be shaken. They yearn for their return to the haven of home.*"

. . . . .

Removing his hat Arno tucked it under his arm.

Turning, he walked across the platform. Passed the monument. Walked to steps that would take him into the field of crosses . . .

Row upon row of crosses. All white crosses as far as he could see . . .

Arno took the slip of paper from the pocket of his uniform, looked down and studied the numbers. Somewhere here they said he'd find him—

"It's me Ted. It's Arno—"

HE WALKS BESIDE US

A stirring of air, belying presence,
Bringing strength to courage,
Love to the midst of challenge,
Smoothing the rough way,
With His peaceful silence.

He shares our burden,
In the warmth of a handclasp,
With a touch of magic,
Called forth as love,
Smoothing well-worn fears,
Into hope steadfast.

His is the mystery,
Beyond understanding,
That peace of completeness,
Uplifting life's journey,
Smoothing heartfelt pain,
Into joy of healing—
Willing us whole.

Love, Laughter and Tears . . .

TANTE MARTINE
Norway April 9, 1940 . . .

OSLO, NORWAY
Viking lore and misty fjords,
Cobble stone streets,
What do they tell us . . .

TANTE MARTINE

Uneasiness settled over her morning and the feeling played with her spirits, and it wouldn't pass. It seemed to Martine it was the same as that day Laurits was killed—the same feeling. It wouldn't go away that day either: *Laurits Heksberg, Oslo Firefighter #698—killed on duty* the papers had said, and little Jenny had been only ten years old. Now Jenny lived in America, in Bemidji, Minnesota, and Martine was seventy-two—and alone.

Pushing back the curtain she looked out at gentle snowflakes that hid their valley and hills beyond. And there was a snowy white cap sitting on the gatepost, the last snowfall of a bitter winter. It didn't help her restlessness. *We would be skiing . . .* she knew for sure . . . *or snowshoeing . . . sure I tenk* (think) *it looks good for snowshoes.*

Then the more Martine thought of a nice fire in the kitchen fireplace with the smell of lefsa bread baking, the more an idea took hold, . . . *why not go down to Bjorn's and get flour for lefsa? Tenk, Tenk pä det! Kos Meg.* (Think. Think about that! Be cozy.)

Pulling on boots and jacket, she began fishing the bottom of the kitchen closet for a lost leather mitten. One of those with fur lining—her favorites. But at that moment the bell on her gate gave out a furious ringing. Martine peered up at her clock—*seven–forty?* Too early for neighbors she was sure. But turning back to the window she smiled. Running up the garden path was her niece Anna who often drove down to shop in these quaint villages southeast of Oslo.

Now how I wish I'd baked lefsa bread earlier, Martine scolded herself. Then watching Anna she felt pleasure turn to alarm, couldn't get to the door before her niece almost rang the buzzer off the wall!

"Anna, for goodness sakes—?"

"Tante (aunt) Martine! Oh, thank the Good Lord you're home. I'd visions of looking all over the village!"

"I was just going to Bjorn's store—"

"You've got to come! You just must Tante Martine! Right now! To Lillistrome. So get things together— I've . . ." Anna could go no further, but leaned against the door bursting into tears—

"Oh, Martine . . . it's just terrible—horrible—so horrible! I'm so awful frightened!"

"What on earth child! What is this Anna?"

"The bombing! Bombing Bergen! Germany attacking! We've got to hurry—where's your suitcase? Find . . . ," Anna stared, her words shifting incoherently in the face of Martine's dazed expression. Suddenly she realized *Martine didn't know* —

"Oh, of course! There's no radio!"

"Bombing Bergen? Our lovely Bergen? Hitler!" Martine was suddenly grateful for a nearby chair.

"It's happening," sobbed Anna, "Nazi on the coast and Oslo soon won't be safe. Not even southeast far as this—so you've got to come north to Lillistrome! Niles found out at the lumber mill and they sent all the men to home. He's got the children. Has gone out to bury our Bible and valuables on the back mountain."

Martine shook her head. Tried to think. "Anna, I can't just walk out of my home. I'll need to gather . . . things . . . clothes . . . some things—"

"You've got to come! I don't know how much time we have Tante Martine."

"Lillistrome won't be any safer, Anna. There will be no place safe. Only Sweden."

"Sweden . . . ?"

Anna stared. "Oh, you mean their neutrality..."

On her feet now, Martine looked around her. This house had been in her Berntsen family for generations. Except for her younger sister Jorgine and herself, all her brothers and sisters had left for America so many years ago . . . *Oh how glad I am that Jenny's safe in Minnesota*— And turning back to Anna she said:

"Anna, my Laurits and I chose to stay in Norway. I love our country. And I'm proud of our brave, brave people. Every winter we skied our mountains and on days like this I still snowshoe the trails, still come back for coffee in the kitchen . . . "

"Martine! Martine please—"

"Anna—? Oh . . . of course. I'm rambling," Martine turned away. "Anna dear, you go home to your family. They need you. I'll pack some things and drive up soon." Removing her parka jacket Martine laid it on the kitchen table.

Anna couldn't believe it! Feisty, stubborn Martine—still a skier—still on snowshoes, and living alone . . . *but this is a matter of staying alive,* she almost blurted out. Then perplexed . . . staring at Martine, Anna reconsidered, s*omehow it sounded right.*

"I love you Martine, . . . I'm just terribly afraid—"

Taking Anna into her arms, Martine reached beyond her own fright to stroke the smooth dark head that lay against her, "I love you, Anna, you've been a daughter to me. *And yes, it's fearsome. We must be very, very careful."*

"Niles and I will come back for you this afternoon Tante Martine. He can drive your car. But hurry!"

"Yes, you do that. And I'll be sure to be ready."

With misgivings, Anna closed the gate behind her. She turned the car north toward Lillistrome, *she'll get Niles. For sure Niles will get Martine to come* . . . easily they could be back by three o'clock...

Anna's foot hit the pedal to the floor and the little car responded in a burst of petrol. *God willing it will be in time*, she prayed...

Martine walked through the rooms of the only home she had ever known, grown up in, lived in with Laurits, *Jenny was a baby here.* Some treasures couldn't be left behind. She had sent most with Jenny—but photos—there were still photos. Martine picked up the cross Laurits had given her . . . struggling to put it on with shaking fingers.

Nazi soldiers! She shuddered. What she had feared most—*Hitler's army in Norway!*

She forced herself not to panic—

"Clothes," she told herself firmly, *she would need clothes.* Going to her chest she began to choose carefully—talking aloud as was her habit, "Warm sturdy clothes . . . yes, and take the food. Get my coat. These I'll wear—" And gathering an armful Martine carried ski pants, wool sweaters and socks to the kitchen dumping them on the table beside her parka jacket. Then—

"Skis and snowshoes—mine and Laurits' both. I'll have to get them from the shed—hurry, hurry!"

She was moving now.

Rap, rap . . . rap, rap . . . A sudden play of knuckles on the kitchen door made her jump!

"Bjorn! Oh Bjorn! Come in quickly. "

"Close your drapes, Martine, I was passing and noticed they were open." As he spoke Bjorn was walking through every room lowering shades—turned off a light—then another . . .

"And no lights. Don't you have candles? A flashlight?"

Martine flushed, "Yes, yes of course."

Bjorn looked at her, "Afraid?"

"Oh min Gud yes, Bjorn. I am that—!"

"Ya, so is everyone. Over the wireless they tell us the German paratroopers have landed in Stavanger—the airport," said Bjorn.

He continued to stare at her until suddenly Martine grew uncomfortable:

"Bjorn?"

"Martine, your Jenny is in America. So is our son Lars—so we are dangerous to the Nazi. People like us they consider spies, Martine. You, Astrid and myself, we are in great danger. Martine we've got to get to Sweden."

Speechless, Martine sat down trying to take it all in. All coming so fast, *Bergen—Anna—Nazi invasion and now…*

"I was Laurits' closest friend, Martine. Astrid and I have tried to look out for you—"

"And I'm grateful…"

"Martine we *must* get to Sweden. Do you think you can snowshoe? You know the trail. It's only seven kilometers to the border. There may be trains, but Nazi can inspect those. In this snow we'll have to use snowshoes."

"When?"

"Soon— Now—very soon. Our only chance."

Everything seemed to come clear for her, . . . Martine thought of Anna's contempt for Sweden's declared neutrality . . . *was there any other choice? Could she get to Jenny?* She pushed thoughts of Anna's family aside, *Anna will be safe.* But she, Bjorn and Astrid— *Of course!*

"Martine?"

Bjorn came over and patted her shoulder, "Martine? "

"I'm strong, Bjorn. I just took that trail last week," Martine smiled at his sigh of relief.

"Two o'clock, Martine. I'll carry bread and coffee in my pack, and a blanket. Two o'clock. Astrid and I will meet you at the trailhead —*Two o'clock*, Martine."

Martine nodded, "Two o'clock."

Bjorn had the door open. Turned back. "Papers, Martine, you'll need your papers."

"I'll be ready, Bjorn."

"So lock this door. Stay away from windows."

After listening to the gate bell Martine took deep breaths, scolded: "Mustn't panic, no panic, . . . *forget packing! Get snowshoes!* And taking down the key she left for the old shed behind the house.

It was in returning that Martine heard something she did not understand . . . *Tenk! . . . Tenk! . . . Somehow she knew the sound . . . yet could not place it?*

The snow had stopped. The air was still.

The sound . . . *like a dull echo* . . . seemed to be coming from under the mists rolling in from Oslo fjord—

She waited—

When it came again—the sound brought a **chill!** *She shivered! What was it?* Martine peered out toward the road. . . . Suddenly she remembered! —*Marching! Troops marching in step!*

She hurried inside and locked the door.

Twenty minutes past ten o'clock . . . Time for a sandwich and a cup of tea. Then taking down her tin box of family photos, she sat down to write . . . *first a letter for her precious Jenny.* Then a note for Anna . . . *dear Anna and Niles with all those beautiful children.*

Twelve o'clock, time to dress . . . . She began putting on layers of clothing, smoothing them over a slim, firm body. Last came the parka jacket, snow goggles going in one pocket, flashlight in another. A sealskin packet of papers and money she fastened to an inside pocket. Then instinctively Martine reached up to wind her clock.

It was one o'clock...

"Goodbye my home," she whispered... "It will take all I can give..." —*But I can do it!* She brushed away tears she could not afford to shed, thinking... *Laurits would be proud of me."*

Mist was settling into Norway's dusky–pale afternoon when she secured her gate before crossing the road to a path that led to the trailhead.

Bending down, Martine felt for tough leather straps on the snowshoes. Fastened them quickly to her boots.

Readied, she leaned forward on her poles...

Listened—

Heard only a misty silence. And the mist was comforting.

Slup... sup, Slup... a–sup...

The quietness of snowshoes was something to love. Working her poles Martine set an easy, steady pace—

Slup... sup, Slup... a–sup... Slup... sup...

It will be no different from any other time on the trail. Less than seven kilometers, and at every stop a rest hut, a*nd with good people,* she told herself—

Slup... sup, Slup... a–sup... Slup... sup...

On the same trail two weeks before she had looked over into Sweden seeing Norway's brave Home Guards on duty... .*Now she would go further... leave her beloved Norway—*

"Dear Gud, help my Norway..." The words brought tears—

—*But I'll return. I will return!*

Swinging into the lane before the trailhead she stopped to wipe her eyes. Took a fresh grip on her poles. Ahead through rising mist two figures looked like Bjorn and Astrid.

"Well," Martine almost shouted, "I'm ready. Let's go."

· · · · ·

When Anna and Niles pulled up in front of the house a dull-red glow flooded the skies over Oslo. In the misty grayness of Norway's winter afternoon Martine's village was strangely quiet.

Anna felt uneasy.

Then she realized Niles had already knocked twice, and took out her key.

"Maybe she's asleep," said Niles. "Stay here." After circling to the kitchen he returned.

"Everything's closed up, Anna, I don't think she's here."

Anna gasped! "Must be! Tante promised." Following Niles she walked into a frightening silence—.

"Tante Martine?"

"She's not here Anna."

"Martine—?" Anna took in the disarray of Martine's bedroom.

Niles frowned, "Just a hunch, I'm going to check the shed."

Overcome with trembling, Anna sat down at the kitchen table. And finding both matches and a stub of candle—she lit it— stared at a lovely, rosemaling painted box with her name on it. The box lay open on the table when Niles returned with two pairs of skis—

"Anna her snowshoes are gone!" He shook his head in disbelief, "I have her and Laurits' skis."

Anna looked up—

"Photos, Niles," she whispered . . ."In this box . . . photos of my mother and my grandparents. There's an envelope for Jenny and a note . . . it's for us,"

Anna handed the note to him—

"Where is she, Niles? What's . . ."

Niles gasped in disbelief…

"The good Lord help her! I just can't . . ." he began… But the look of pain that flashed across Anna's face stopped him cold—

"Niles, this note on Jenny's envelope!" Anna read aloud:

> ... *Anna—Please mail this when you can, when Norway is free again. I love you, —Martine*

Struggling to stay calm, Niles shook his head, "She's gone, Anna. She's taken the trail to Sweden on her snowshoes."

They stared at each other trying to comprehend. And seeing an empty cup on the sideboard Niles walked over. He found it was still wet . . . turned to stare at window shades he'd never seen pulled down before. *Uneasiness rose to chilling fear—*

"I'll get the other snowshoes from the shed—Hurry Anna!"

The urgency in his voice did not seem to reach her, as ignoring tears that made it hard to see, Anna moved to snuff-out the candle. Bending down, she picked something up from the floor. Looked more closely? In her hand was the gold cross Uncle Laurits had given Tante Martine! The clasp was broken....

Anna put it in her pocket. She would keep it.

· · · · ·

"This is Norway Free Radio - April 9, 1940
— Germany is attacking us —
***Repeat*— Germany is attacking us!"**
Norway Free Radio - fell silent until 1945.

· · · ·

Every day Anna wrote in her diary:
—We are betrayed by treacherous Vidkun Quisling and secret Nazi. —We hear shooting from the trails now. —No longer dare to use trails. —Teachers arrested today! Neighbors disappeared. —Maybe to concentration in Germany? —Told there are camps even here, somewhere. In Norway! —Imagine! —Oh Martine, dearest Tante Martine, where are you?!

Then at Niles' warning, Anna burned her diary.

And in Bemidji, Minnesota, in the United States of America, Jenny and her family prayed daily for her mother.

"I've had no word," Jenny replied to a call from her cousin, Violet Hansen.

"*And with Norway liberated, for more than a year*," mused Vi.

"And we know the Red Cross is trying . . . but we haven't learned anything, Violet. —Nothing."

Jenny's worry was compounded by her husband's new job in Oregon, and the imminent move, *how ever will Martine find them?*

Trudging out to their mailbox through the first snowfall, Jenny wiped tears and stray flakes away before pulling open the box. Then she blinked, took a breath . . . *a little string–tied package? A postmark: Norway!*

Tearing it open, inside were two envelopes and a little packet—

Her shouts brought husband Leo to her side—

"Leo! Leo! From Mother! A letter from my mother!"

Then sitting beside him Jenny *whispered:*

". . . But it's old, Leo . . . it's old . . . "

A note was dated: April 9, 1940.

My beloved datter Jenny,

My first prayers are for Norway, for wonderful Norway, the land of your birth also. Whatever happens to me always remember her proud and brave people in your prayers.

This afternoon I leave for Sweden. I will snowshoe from the trailhead with good friends. It is only seven kilometers (less than 4 miles for you). I am very strong so do not worry. The Lord willing, I will be with you before you get this. Whatever happens, I love you always. I am so glad you and Leo, and my grandchildren are safe.

— Mother

When Jenny could not go on Leo read a letter aloud:

October 10, 1946 *— Lillistrome, Norway.*

Dearest cousin Jenny,

I am Selma, your cousin Anna's oldest daughter. After so much, it has taken time to adjust and send this note to you. When the Nazi invaded, my Anna and Niles went to fetch out Tante Martine, but she was gone. My mother had found this note for you.

Also, this gold cross was on the floor in Tante's kitchen, and mother told me Uncle Laurits had given it to Tante who always wore it. Mother thought Martine might have lost it because the clasp is broken. Now I think you should have it.

In a note to my parents Tante said she was fleeing to Sweden on snowshoes and I know a trail to the border begins close to her home. Dearest cousin, I am sorry, but we have no news. Martine's name is not on any refugee or prison lists. You may hear before we do. Please write. My love to you and your family. Please pray for us. — Selma.

With a mug of fresh coffee in hand . . . *sipping slowly* . . . Jenny moved aside the kitchen curtain . . . stood looking out at gently swirling snowflakes that hi, d their road, the wooded hills beyond. There was a snowy white cap sitting on the gatepost . . . *so like home in Norway.*

Jenny smiled . . . *It was good seeing it there.*

Leo's voice healed the silence, "Your mother was a patriot and very brave, Jenny."

"And I must always think of her that way," whispered Jenny.

YOU ARE WITH ME STILL

You are gone my love away,
Yet with me still,
I hear a step in the passageway,
Hold here in mine a loving hand,
You are gone my love away.
Yet with every dawning,
When night mists fade, and
I walk the warmth of ocean sands,
There comes a gentle sound,
From dunes and hill,
A sweet wind whispering,
And you are with me still.

Love, Laughter and Tears . . .

TO AMERICA

Though mists of time they came,
Those who sought better life in a land unknown,
By ship to the shores they came,
By boat with paddle, on foot they came,
By horse and carriage, by wind, by train,
Lumbermen, farmers, ministers, girl of sixteen.

Through mists of memory we see them,
Those who found seeds of life in that hard land,
Who with hardy courage forged existence,
Those whose children we are, begot and raised.

For love of freedom so prayed for,
Through mist of time they came,
Those who sought a life in a land unknown,
Enriching our souls with courage.

A COUNTESSA *and the* CARPENTER
A Novella . . .

Olympia Catharina
1879-1963

Massimo Michael
1874-1960

A COUNTESSA *and the* CARPENTER

I

Watching her he saw such beauty it was a struggle within to remain silent. Here was a vision of loveliness he had never seen the like of before . . . sunlight playing over porcelain–fair cheek and parted lips, waves of curls tumbling to her waist. Unseen, Massimo watched. As swaying gently on the bench, the girl twisted her hair, and with one motion, secured it high with golden combs, the violet silk of her dress slipping easily over firm breasts. And smoothing the silken folds over her hips, turning, seeing him, her eyes flashed—large brown eyes that took his breath. She recognized his look, smiled and turned away good–humored. Disappeared into the villa. But not before Mike saw that he pleased her. A spontaneous impression. He was smitten,

A spirited one, he told himself—*Daughter of the house?. . . or who is she?*

She was gone, but the vision of that sweet loveliness remained with all its freshness. he had only to close his eyes to see her again. *He had to find out who she is.* But telling himself, *to be careful* . . . he pulled back to the reality of having been hired to make cupboards for the villa. No job had awaited him in Italy. Starting out alone as a carpenter, he had to make good with the cupboards. Success would only come through his hands—with the skills and talent the good God had given him. Now they were all he had.

He had not wanted to return. It was the shock of Checo's murder in Paris, and the facing of life alone in such a hostile city that decided him. Massimo fondly called Francesco—"Checo." While his brother had always called him "Mike." And returning to Italy, he will call himself—Mike. Working as a builder in Paris with his older brother had held much promise. Still today his brother's murder hurt badly.

He and Checo had been in their street-side, Paris apartment that day—had been sitting across from each other eating lunch in the cool darkness that afforded relief from the city beyond their window. Shutters back, the window had been open to the street allowing enough light to eat by. Soon they would have to return to the building site where Checo's men were hard at work. That was when Mike asked—

"What went wrong this morning Checo?"

Checo shrugged. "You saw Fliipe go steaming?"

"I saw him leaving—Slamming stuff—" said Mike.

"I fired the guy, Mike. Should'a done it a long time ago for all that fighting and what his shoddy work has cost me. I sent him off."

Mike nodded, "In a fury."

"No doubt! Hope we've seen the last of him."

Mike dug into the mound of pasta on his plate, not his favorite food, but what Checo cooked best. So Mike always accepted it. And looking over at Checo, he matched his smile. Looking at his brother was always like looking at their father. They'd both inherited Dominico's flashing eyes, but to Mike, Checo's resemblance to their father was stronger, and studying his brother, Mike took pleasure in the thought.

Checo swiped a napkin across his mouth, and Mike thought he was going to say more when sounds of a scuffle erupted in the street outside. Then a shout! For weeks, workers in Paris had been marching for wages, filling the streets with growing crowds of bitter, hostile men. Checo motioned to the shutters:

"Close the window Mike."

Mike pushed back in his chair. He can remember getting to his feet—walking over to the open window. There had been only an instant glimpse of a gun in a man's hand before the hot bullet *whizzed by nicking his right ear—sped on* through the room's dimness to hit Checo in the head—killing him outright. Blood streaming down his cheek Mike had turned. Stared in horror! January 10, 1897.

Still shaken, grieving, in another week Mike had buried twenty–six year old Checo and was gathering his own things—
What else can I do but leave?

For months he had watched dangerous unrest growing in the streets of Paris. It would be better to go back home to Italy. His father had died when Mike was fourteen. His mother was re–married to someone Mike detested . . . *but what could he do?* He was fond of his sister who was Postmistress in Milano, and there was a half–brother born after he and Checo had left. No other family. But Dominico's workshop was still there in the little hamlet and Mike knew it would be his now as his father's only surviving son. And thinking long and hard, he had come to the conclusion that no one working in the hamlet was as skilled as he was—not in the whole area.

So mourning Checo, trusting in himself . . . Mike had returned to Italy to find that not much had changed in the hamlet those nine years he was away. Nestled in the foothills of Italy's northern Apennines Mountains, the little town was as old as Italy itself—even older. Dominico's shop was in the *Borgo* (lower town) where tradesmen lived and worked, while on a hill above was an "upper town" with its ancient monastery and handsome, spacious villas.

On his twenty-fourth birthday in February Mike was working as a carpenter and soon felt curious heads turning, felt the looks that followed him. Fair of coloring, a tall, slim man with fine features, it was obvious he had considerable strength. But what was noticed first were his unusual eyes, hazel–grey eyes with slices of gold that glinted when he laughed—began shimmering when he grew thoughtful—flashed with insight.

Mike smiled as he walked through the Borgo . . . otherwise ignored the questioning looks that came his way. Opening the shop. Hard at work. He took great pride in being trustworthy, and word began to spread about the young man who worked the wood so lovingly, so creatively with his hands. By March the lathe in his workshop was humming.

That is where he stood one morning working the lathe with doors open, the warmth of sunlight streaming into the shop—when suddenly—a dark shadow fell across the floor. Startled! Mike stopped. Turning, he stared at an imposing figure, *"here was not someone to be ignored."*

"I am told you are a *Master* craftsman?" The bold sonorous voice reverberated through the shop.

"Some will say that," replied Mike.

And spelling for time, flipping a lock on the lathe, Mike began brushing away sawdust all the while taking in trim trousers, a broad crimson waistcoat and smart cut of coat. The man himself was short and solidly built with an aura about him of excellence. But beneath a full mustache, thin lips were pressed closed—unsmiling.

And thinking fast, Mike guessed he knew him. From style and build, this could only be someone he'd heard tell of. The owner of a spacious villa on the hill—Rodosindo, head of a most honored family. Although the hamlet was a small, isolated place, their little town was known throughout Italy as the "Lawyers Town" for its many "illustrious" Men of Law who served the Senate at Roma, *and this Rodosindo is one of them*—Mike was sure, for the man emitted a forceful presence. All this had passed through Mike's mind in seconds.

He took an immediate dislike to Rodosindo. And trusting his instincts, proud of being beholding to no one—when the man stood silent—Mike turned back to his work.

"I have need of you. Now! Immediately!" The voice rose another octave.

At that Mike moved. Pulling all six feet of himself to full height he walked over to the door, and looking down at the man offered his hand—as was done in Paris. His smile turned to a grin when Rodosindo stepped back.

"I expect I'm talking to Rodosindo Andreoli," said Mike.

"So you know me."

"I've been building in Paris a long time, but have heard . . ."

"No matter—" Rodosindo waved that aside. "I want the best workmanship. There is work needs doing at my villa. I want new cupboards throughout and I must have the best."

"As I said, my work is that," replied Mike.

His irritation growing Mike waited. He watched as Rodosindo took in the workshop, the critical stare, ending with Mike's work boots—unwilling to "look up" to a Carpenter.

Mike didn't miss it. He considered the man could be—clever, cunning, absurd, eloquent, *most likely, trouble.*

"Sit down. I will explain," said Rodosindo. Short words. An order. "What's your name? I, . . . so, . . . wasn't your father that wheelwright? You've a half–brother." A furrow creased Rodosindo's brow...

"You look young to be a *Master.*"

"I am Massimo Michael. I am the only living son of Dominico. And if twenty-four appears young—" Eyes flashing Mike spoke firmly, making himself sufficiently clear before walking away with...

"You can get someone else."

"No! I am told you are the best. I always have the best."

Mike swung back to face him. "You will then pay well."

"Of course."

"So—" Mike considered. "So then I will come see for myself. Tomorrow. And after I come. Then I will tell you the lire." He again extended his hand—a gesture ignored. Obviously refused.

That was how it began. Mike often had reason to look back on that meeting and puzzle over his reaction to Rodosindo. Being wise in the ways of men, and having seen something of the world beyond, Mike had always prided himself of not being over-awed by man, wealth, or station of life. That he had acted as he had that early morning, March 1898—had felt cause to do so—left Mike thinking. Later he would call it—*Instinct at work.*

The next morning he approached the villa with conflicting thoughts. But knew the lire would be good. He would make sure of that! And Mike knew a job well done could bring more such work. So when a maid "tartly" ordered him to the back entry, unperturbed, he entered a large kitchen. Within minutes he was measuring, estimating, considering what wood to use, how to bring out the best grain for its beauty, and irritation with Rodosindo faded away. Mike could see the work was indeed considerable—extending throughout the villa. It could take two months, *even longer.* And within two days' time a price was given. Was accepted. So as usually happened when settling in to work he was happy, with his heart in the job in front of him. Soon he was whistling, and having a fine voice he began singing folk songs and snatches of Verdi's arias that he knew well and loved.

Then arriving early one morning, it was from the kitchen door that Mike first saw the girl as she sat combing her hair in the courtyard. And some days later soft footsteps approached where he was working.

Looking up, pulling a sharp breath, Mike asked himself, "How can anyone be so lovely?"

Her voice interrupted his thoughts with, "Who are you?"

"Mike . . . Massimo Michael—and you?"

"Olympia."

"You are—"

"Olympia Catarina." The voice held an unusual firmness. "You are working for my father."

"Oh—" Turning away, Mike picked up rule and pencil.

"You do not like him."

"This villa is imposing—well built," said Mike.

"So is my father," her smile suddenly flashed into delighted laughter. "Show me what you are doing. This wood is beautiful. I do like it. Must it be painted?"

"No—only waxed or oiled to show the grain," said Mike.

Soft, fine–boned fingers traced the fluid grain of the wood as Mike watched and soon he was explaining, enjoying her company.

From that day on he looked forward to seeing Olympia. So it grew between them day upon day as his work at the villa continued. And that was how it began, mutual attraction developing swiftly to love—love understood, but *absolutely* unspoken between them.

Yet Mike knew, *he loved the first moment he saw her*.

He was torn with irresolution—what could he do? He both disliked and distrusted Rodosindo. Besides, he was a carpenter—would be considered far below Olympia, a daughter . . . who with marriage—would surely be a Countessa? He had heard of Olympia's admired brothers – one of the Law – the other a doctor. Olympia was close to her older, married sister Livia, *and above all there was Rodosindo.*

Mike needed help. After much thought he turned to a friend from many years, the son of a vintner. Someone Mike admired for being forthright. Besides . . . he knew that Roberto Mondavi was sweet on Rosa who was the daughter of Olympia's maid.

"Roberto, what do you know?" asked Mike.

Roberto quickly agreed to Mike's caution:

"There's good reason to be concerned Mike. Be very careful—especially until your work is finished. From what my Rosa tells me, yes, she and Olympia may be like sisters in the villa, but with being

Rodocindo's daughter, eighteen–year–old Olympia is the *bell* of villa society. And she is well protected—watched over. Olympia is being squired by every young Duke or Count lucky enough to meet her father's approval as suitable. Papa takes care of the family name."

It was what Mike already suspected and dreaded.

Nonetheless, when Olympia could slip away from her maid she came to watch Mike work.

"Olympia, dear sister—" cautioned Livia, alarmed at what Olympia was telling her . . .

When Olympia pushed on in soft whispers:

"Massimo Michael is decent and well spoken Livia. Besides, he's the most handsome of men. And he's kind. He respects me. Never would Mike try to compromise as Luigi did. Once while walking ahead of me up the hill Luigi turned to pull at my bodice and look down at my breasts."

With Livia won over as confidant, Rosa sworn to secrecy, Olympia and Mike found times to talk walking together beside the river flowing through the hamlet. Rosa following discreetly—as custom demanded. But Mike was very much aware that the river was turning a great wheel in the mill owned by Rodosindo. Only one of the man's many investments and lands. The family's wealth and position was not lost on Mike. He remained cautious. As did Olympia. And in that way the weeks passed until what Mike dreaded—happened. His work at the villa was completed.

Olympia knew, with a deep honesty, *I will never love anyone as much as I love my Mike.* It became her last thought when falling asleep—her first words to greet every new morning. Olympia also knew—more than anyone. More than Mike even, *Papa loves me too much . . . too much!* And as September days passed into October she began slipping from the villa early mornings to walk hillside paths with trusted Rosa—thinking—thinking. Asking herself, "Is there a way? *There will be a way! Must be!"* . . .

I will never love anyone as much as I love my Mike.

Then she knew—

In the warmth of an October evening, sitting side–by–side with Mike on a bench near the river, she sensed Mike's heart–felt, yet unspoken words. And placing a hand on Mike's arm—Olympia spoke for herself:

"Father will never consent to marriage."

"I must still ask—" Mike held his breath.

"Only after I tell him *first,*" said Olympia. "But it will not *ever* matter, my Mike. I will marry you."

"You have my love and my promise Olympia. I dearly cherish you with all my heart," Mike grew silent . . . spoke gently:

"Still you know it is expected. I must ask—"

Olympia put a finger to his lips and shook her head. Then rising to go said again:

"I must tell him first Mike. Papa loves too much."

Watching her move away down the river path, Mike felt a flood of relief—joy tempered with knowing that he must speak for himself, custom demanded it . . . *he had to ask Rodosindo for his daughter's hand in marriage.*

Olympia had shared something precious. The silence that rose with her leaving soon filled with bird songs as Mike sat thinking—watching as the sun set—until silence finally made him restless and he made his way home by light of a full moon. A few days later Mike approached the villa and confronted Rodosindo only to come away in a *fury*—spurned—insulted by father and both brothers.

But determined, now fully confident of Olympia's love, Mike bicycled over the hills to visit his sister in Milano and purchased a wide ring of gold.

Being caught unawares, it was while Mike was gone that Rodosindo pulled himself stiffly upright overcome with rage. The furor that broke over the head of Olympia had rarely been heard in the family—never in Rodosindo's lifetime:

"Not ever! Not from our very beginnings!" he raged.

Nothing appeared to phase Olympia. Having anticipated his arguments, back rigid, head high, she fought back. Eyes flooded with tears snapped with defiance in the presence of all opposition to the astonishment of both Rodosindo and her mother Maria…

"What do I care for your sacredness of *custom* Papa! Of marrying as you say, *below* my station? I must live for myself—my own nature—not ancient ideas," argued Olympia.

"You will marry who I say! And with title!" shouted Rodosindo.

"I will have My Mike!" declared Olympia.

On Mike's return she fled to him, with Mike comforting her as well as he could with incredible tenderness.

But as Olympia had determined, her father's fury was made all the worse by her being not only the youngest of his children, but the *favored* one. Rodosindo turned on her:

"Marry the son of a wheelwright! You would marry such? A carpenter? So below us! Bring shame to our name! *Never* Olympia Catarina! Such is forbidden—unforgivable of you!" shouted Rodosindo. And he turned in wrath upon his wife:

"Get your daughter to see reason Maria Sadore!"

And seeing her mother in agreement! In spite of Maria's weeping Olympia rose to hot defiance—

"I will have My Mike! You are in conspiracy against him! Massimo Michael is a good man, unbiased, un-bribable by you Papa and your traditions." Olympia spoke firmly.

"No!" Rodosindo's voice thundered throughout the villa, "Has he courted you honorably? Come to me, your father—for permission first? No!"

And pulling from deep within herself Olympia brought forth the best ammunition she could think of—that same pride of family and honor that had been impressed upon her since childhood:

"*You*, Papa, have denied him," said Olympia. "You have taught me that *nothing* is sacred but family integrity—well that is not so! I love Mike and he loves me. *Love too is sacred Papa*. I only ask that you accept us."

"Never!" swore Rodosindo. "Go to your good–natured carpenter! Live his mode of life if you will—without my or your mother's blessing."

"That I marry the man I love is all that concerns me Papa. I love Massimo Michael with all my heart and soul—"

Olympia spun on her heel and left the villa. Refused to return. Approached by Livia—by her brothers—she repelled all words of doom.

"I have decided," said Olympia.

November 25, 1898 being her nineteenth birthday, She rose early and dressed with care before stepping out into warm sunshine to take Mike's hand. Side–by–side they walked to a tiny, ancient chapel where tall floor tapers cast a soft, golden glow over the ancient, white marble altar and painting of Rafael's "Madonna," when she and her Mike were joined in holy matrimony. Rosa and Roberto standing beside them. They wrote carefully in the church book:

Olympia Catarina - Nineteen years.
Massimo Michael - Twenty-four years.

At twelve–o'clock–noon, Rodosindo Andreoli walked into the Borgo's center plaza and ordered the town bells, "Be rung," as he publicly disowned his youngest daughter.

Undaunted, Olympia and Mike moved into rooms over the workshop. Then what they knew would happen—*did.* Citizens of the hamlet reacted in shocked anger!

And Mike stormed—shook his fist: "Respect for Rodosindo? Disapproval? Fear of reprisal! It's that—and more!"

The reaction was vicious. People gathering in villas. Gathering in houses of the Borgo. Hostile groups standing in the Marketplace. Mike and Olympia being shunned in public.

Only Roberto, Rosa and Olympia's sister Livia dared befriend them—and then in secret. Every shout and stare is hurtful.

A furious Livia warned, "There is no way to begin to set them right but to meet their taunts with a forced smile."

"So!" said Olympia, "then we will treat it as a trifle, be decorous and prudent."

And fortified with Mike's strength, drawing upon the courage of breeding and dignity expected of her by family, she rose to the challenge. Holding her tongue, straightening her back, Olympia walked with pride at Mike's side. Both ignoring insults the best they could. It wasn't easy—not even when the most vicious gossipers were growing tired. Over many months a thin peace settled over Mike's shop. But self-dependent and working hard, Mike's business was growing. And Olympia welcomed Mike's family into her life.

When Rosa asked—

Olympia replied, "If this is the way it's going to be, I will not bow or apologize."

II

Over the next six years Olympia gave birth to each of their children in the small "birthing room" within the house of Massimo Michael's mother. A daughter was born October 1899 and named Estella. A son in September 1901 to be called John Domenic for Mike's father, and second daughter Angela in August 1902. October 1903 a second son is born, and taking the newborn into his arms, Massimo Michael names him "Francesco," for his brother Checo . . .

"We'll call him Frank," said Mike.

Married six years, and all the while Olympia knows she was right. She has found her own happiness with Massimo Michael who she continues to call *My Mike*. And when he begins calling her "My *Mimi (little one)*" —Olympia quickly adopts it:

" . . . *Mimi* I will be from now on."

For Mike every child is his treasure. Pedaling over the hills to visit his sister in Milano two-year-old John is usually seated on the front of Mike's bike. When the children are taken to the river Summer afternoons, Mike is leaping into the water with a child on his back, while Mimi sits wondering if shrill shouts of delight might be reaching her mother in the villa.

No matter. Cruel gossip and ugly stares continue. And in his concern for her, whenever Mike asks . . . Mimi replies—

"Every day . . . every walk to the marketplace is difficult."

The coming of winter always brought a change in living, when mountains hold snow and rivers can become ice-bound. But even before little Frank was born that October, Mike had sensed something else . . . *his concern growing*. In Milano milling crowds were uneasy. Unrest was spreading. The streets of Roma were teaming with scenes of fighting, men organizing, chanting, marching with placards—brass horns blowing. Mike knew of only one person he could trust who might have news from Roma—Roberto Mondavi.

Returning at dusk one afternoon the two of them met near the market where Mike pulled Roberto into the deepest shadows, keeping his voice low:

"Roberto we need to talk." said Mike. "People in Milano tell me they are more and more uneasy . . . and not just for Italy. And now unrest is growing in Roma—coming North, closer. I'm worried Roberto."

"And I was just at your shop—missing you," whispered Roberto, "It's *more* than something to be nervous about, Mike. There's dangerous anger. I don't like what I hear."

Mike considered, "I'm thinking Marxists, a push for—"

"More—" Roberto interrupted. "Today I got a warning from Roma. There's danger to this—*for us Mike.*"

Mike felt his jaw tighten, "I'm remembering what happened in Paris—to Checo."

"And I'm serious about America Mike."

Mike nodded, "It's in my mind too. It's been bad here. Especially for Mimi," he whispered, "and there are my children—"

"Is Mimi willing?"

"I . . . we've only talked . . . we haven't—"

"Mike, we are right to fear for our skins. I'm not going to wait it out. *Can you?* It might be too late if we're ordered—"

"You're thinking *conscription*?"

"Aren't you?"

Mike stared at the intense face barely visible in the growing darkness. "Now I am . . . come to the shop, we'll talk."

"I'll be there tomorrow—early."

Deep in thought, firm strides carried Mike rapidly through the Borgo. All around him dusk was settling into first feelings of darkness, soft winds off the foothills moving a veil of white over ancient pavings . . . first sign of snow. Mike shivered, pulling his jacket closer. Tugged at the grey lambs–wool cap Mimi made for him. Concerned, he mulled over Roberto's words, *growing more sure than ever*. Suddenly he stopped. Swung around and could barely make out the rose-tinted walls lining both sides of the narrow street—houses as ancient as the hamlet, and with people inside he didn't understand anymore.

That night he confided in Mimi:

"We've been wondering about America, what it might demand of us . . . now I'm sure Mimi. There is going to be serious, even fateful danger. What if we left Mimi? Went to America. Left Italy. How hard would it be for us? For you?"

Mimi took her time in answering. When she did:

"I think it's not the going Mike—it's where. It's what would you do, Mike? How to live?"

"I am confident Mimi. I was a builder in Paris, a good builder. America must need good builders."

Looking up at him Mimi smiled. She knew he was a good builder, *hasn't he proved It, her Mike?*

Moving to the window she was hardly aware of the dark, deserted streets of the Borgo. Instead, looking toward the villa, she saw foothills bathed silver by a cold moon . . . drew a quiet breath . . . *America? But America was so far . . . still how good was it here?* It wasn't a new feeling. But now, looking down at baby Frank the thought persisted, *how good will it be here for him? For Estella? John? My little Angelina?*

"Mario has gone already—a winemaker," said Mike, "Sante Forte too," he looked over at Mimi. "They went together."

"They had no children Mike," Mimi turned from the window.

"I'm thinking of *our* children Mimi."

"And I think of us Mike. You a builder. Me. So if we go—we go now when we are strong Mike. And if you go first—" Eyes flashing Mimi gave him that beautiful smile:

"Yes we can do it Mike."

"I must go soon Mimi."

"Soon . . . yes, I know," Mimi nodded. Waited.

"Roberto Mondavi is begging me to sail with him, and I think it will be good to go with such a friend. Roberto and I think alike," said Mike.

"Roberto! But he's to marry Rosa—"

"He will come back for her Mimi. When I come for you and the children, Roberto and I will come together."

"Ah . . . so . . . then I wonder? Maybe Rosa will live with me. I'm strong, but that would be good. I won't be alone with children."

"Talk it with her Mimi," Mike spoke quickly. "I'll feel better too, if she's here. But she must be quiet about this."

"I trust Rosa, Mike . . . we are like sisters."

"So go talk to her."

One week later, bowed in disbelief and grief, they buried two-year-old Angela who in three days, died of sudden fever. So now, *no matter what it will take*—even as she nursed Frank at her breast—through her tears Mimi urged Mike to go:

"Mike—my Mike—go Mike! See what you can make of it. Tell me how it is. And when you find something for us I will come with the children. Rosa too."

Livia was horrified. It took many days for Mimi to calm her with promises to write, *and often.* Then fearful of her family she swore Livia to secrecy. No word must reach Papa Rodocindo until Mike has left.

Two weeks later it was still October when Massimo Michael kissed Mimi and his children good-by. Slipping quietly from the hamlet with Roberto, they boarding a train for Roma and sailed for America.

III

"Good-by my Mimi—my little ones . . ."

Mike had only whispered, but even over the noise of ship Roberto recognized the emotion in those words and shared the same feelings . . .

"We're in this together Mike."

"Whatever we find, we will make it good," Mike told him.

With Italia fading away in the distance Mike looked at the man beside him. Facing this unexpected turn his life was taking, he felt good about being with Roberto. He knew him to be honest, and having grown up together best of friends Mike was sure he could rely on Roberto's judgment.

After eight days of ocean they were following the advice of Sante Forte who had gone that way two years before, which meant that instead of New York, Mike found himself disembarking in Philadelphia, to a dark pier smelling of machine oil, fish, and worse—

it was pouring rain. Ominous rolls of thunder brought such a deluge that they found it hard to see where they were going. Satchel in each hand, his tall frame bent almost double, Mike followed Roberto—fighting furious gusts of wind—sloshing through wet, flooding streets searching for a rooming house.

One long month later they were still walking the streets of Philadelphia. Skies were smoky–dark, streets dirty, and lines for jobs were long with nothing to offer at the end. 1903 it seemed everyone needed work.

"No damn jobs! Only for coal miners," swore Roberto.

"I refuse to descend into the bowels of the earth!" Mike thundered.

"This is a strange place, Mike. *It bothers me . . .*"

"Roberto, all I see on faces are *looks of empty hope.*"

Living in one room, sharing what they had . . . Roberto was hopeful. Mike determined. Already fluent in French and Italian, Mike began to spend nights learning to speak and read English. And in Italy with the children Mimi saw winter come to the Apennines as a "White Widow," whose husband in America was sending money to live on. And when Mike wrote . . .

Mimi answered carefully:

. . . so my Mike, it's good here. We are waiting for Spring . . .

"More rain! Every day rain!" Muttering in every language he knew—some he didn't . . . Mike took the three flights to their room doing two steps at a time. Flinging open the door he slammed it with his fist—hard! Hair dripping. Shivering. . .! He stared across the room at Roberto—

Roberto shook his head . . ."No! No luck. Nothing! There's absolutely nothing—nowhere!"

"Worst day yet!" growled Mike. "I've got to bring Mimi and the children next summer—no longer. I need work! This is impossible!" Grabbing a towel, rubbing his wet head, he sat down to unlace his boots.

"Sure no good Mike."

Walking over to the table Roberto flipped a switch under the coffee and began pacing . . . pacing . . . pacing . . . suddenly swung around . . .

Mike looked up— "What?"

"Thinking," said Roberto.

"You've been listening to someone again," said Mike.

"To Sante Forte. He's here seeing a cousin, and from what he says, Minnesota–north doesn't sound so bad Mike. Forte has it figured pretty good I think."

"Minnesota–north? That's terrible cold! Forte told us about"—

"But it's sure no good here Mike. I know grapes and vineyards. I need a place to make money!"

"Minnesota – so far north? Are you crazy Roberto!"

Stripping off his wet clothes Mike hopped around getting into something warm.

"Crazy? So maybe—" mused Roberto.

And picking up Mike's boots, he carried them to the radiator, put them down beside his own, before pouring two cups of coffee. Then handing a cup to Mike, he sat down at the table—

"Maybe crazy Mike . . . but I'm thinking . . . small towns . . . chance to build for you. And me . . . I've got to go back, marry Rosa and bring her too! "

Roberto started pacing again. Stopped in front of Mike: "I need to settle Mike. I miss Rosa. I need my woman."

"*I dunno* . . . ," mused Mike. "Minnesota – so far north?"

But it started Mike thinking. And with coffee warming his insides he lay down still thinking—shook his head:

"Okay Roberto . . . so go find Forte. Let's talk to him."

IV

December 3, 1903 Mike wrote Mimi:

Dear little Mimi, I've got to Minnesota – far north okay. The train stopped for milk cans all night to Chicago. Another train took us to a place, Duluth, on your map. The last train took us further north through woods to a little town—end of the line. Now I am settled-in. Yes, Roberto is with me. Yes there is much snow. Cold. But nice country with hills you will like Mimi. I am busy starting building. Your letter was good little Mimi. I miss you and my children. —your Mike.

What Mike wrote to Mimi was so. Jumping from a train at Virginia the last, most northern stop before Canada, he had walked down a slippery, very frozen, wood sidewalk past a string of steamy, noisy saloons, looking for what someone called, "Our only hardware store." And using his French, what English he knew—Italian thrown in for sure—Mike bought his first tools: hammer, saw, and a spike bar. Inquiring about jobs they walked fifteen miles through the woods to a mining town with a strange name. And eager to be building, by the end of February Mike has built a stone house. By the end of April, Eveleth, Minnesota has its first brick building.

Then Mike bought himself a bicycle and sat down to think, *being my own boss is something new.* As he saw it, *fate had directed things in Italy, some good, some bad . . . Checo, his little Mimi and the children, America, and now this place in good country.*

"But no more," he told himself. It was becoming obvious that in America he could control what happened to him. All he had to do was find a way to do more building so he could have Mimi and the children here by September, a *good feeling!*

Getting to his feet, he kicked around in the red dust for his hammer, grabbed a handful of nails.

"Hey, Mike! My boss is look'in for ya'!"

Mike looked up.

"You're Mike Lenci . . .?"

"I am Mike—sure..."

"Mr. Peteli . . . he's look'in for ya'—down in that shed they use for an office."

"Okay . . . thanks."

Curious . . . pocketing the nails, Mike shook sawdust from his pants before heading for the shed wondering, *what this Peteli guy wants?*

And Mr. Peteli turned out to be a very short, muscular man with curly brown hair, a brush mustache, and above it smiling eyes. Mike put out his hand and introduced himself.

Mr. Peteli gave a hearty handshake, "Hey Mike!" He stepped back to take in Mike's height—and to his surprise, Peteli laughed—

"Yup, you're the man—know you anyplace."

And what Joe Peteli said next had Mike listening hard:

"Mike, I've seen the houses you build and I damn-sure like that kind'a work. I got an offer for you. I need a good man Mike. I want you to come with me on my new job. You'll be working for the Mining Company. Good steady work Mike. Maybe I can even get you some building." Joe Peteli waited . . . let it sink in—

"How 'bout it?"

Feeling his heart start to race, fast as lightening Mike said, "Sound's good Mr. Peteli—where?"

"Mountain Iron."

"Mountain Iron!" Mike sucked in his breath. "Mr. Peteli, Isn't that a far-long ways? Clear the other side of Virginia!"

"Right. Most of my work is gonna' be over there," said Peteli.

Giving a low whistle Mike swore under his breath. . .

Joe Peteli smiled, "Offer stands Mike. Think it over and come see me Friday. *No later.*"

Bicycling home from work that night Mike had some serious thinking to do. He had no car. He knew no one who did. *Bicycle to*

Mountain Iron? He'd done the dirt road to Virginia once—two hours and all up-hill. How far was it from there to Mountain Iron? *Plenty far,* . . . Mike was sure.

There was no sign of Roberto, *so he'll eat alone.* And digging around in the refrigerator, finding half a baloney sandwich, he poured a glass of vino and sat chewing . . . considering the whole idea. Going over it carefully. Especially what Joe Peteli said about building. By nine o'clock it was dark when he put grounds in the pot for morning coffee and turned in. He had until Friday to decide.

Midnight—Mike sat up. —*Forte! What was it Forte told him? A one-car train? On rails?* Didn't Forte say a one-car train used to carry miners through the woods—went between the mining towns? Mike was sure. He was also sure those rails would be long gone, *but wouldn't a path still be there?* Mike had a good idea where that path would be—

His feet hit the floor.

It was still dark, still moonlight, when he pulled out his bike. Three hours later first light of morning was playing over his back when he rode out of pine woods onto a road, and in front of him a sign read:

MOUNTAIN IRON — STRAIGHT AHEAD.

Swiping a hand across his face, wiping away grime, dirt and sweat, Mike knew he'd been lucky—hadn't met a bear, *but that didn't mean there wasn't any! Just luck!* And swinging the bike around it was a hard push back to Eveleth. And come winter? Then he'd have to walk it.

"Roberto! I got to move!"

"Not without me you don't!" Roberto stared, "so we're in this together. Where you go—we go."

"Good," Mike grinned, "to Mountain Iron."

"What!"

"Mountain Iron."

"That's what I thought you said—*and you think I'm crazy*! "

"It's good work, Roberto." By September—you, Rosa, me, Mimi and children will be living in the house you and me are going to build," said Mike.

And with that, Mike was asleep . . . didn't wake until a battered, two-door coupe pulled up—horn blasting!

"Bought it cheap," said Roberto. "No bike for me."

"Sounds like a *dying hen*," said Mike.

Roberto had no retort for that.

Three days later, riding into the village of Mountain Iron with bags and tools strapped to the bike—Mike took one look at a two-street village plastered with red, iron-ore mud, and mighty huge ore trucks—

He'd made a terrible mistake!

There were two wood houses, black chard remains of others, and a burned-out shell of a store—not much else. Fire had swept away everything else! Mike closed his eyes. Opened them. Scratched his head, looked again. Taking a deep breath he changed his mind,

. . . Things were looking up . . . *this means building!*.

"A dang optimist!" swore Roberto when he drove in.

Searching, finding one deserted lot, Mike wondered if it belonged to anyone and went to find Peteli—

"Dunno . . . no one knows, Mike," said Joe Peteli.

Picking up a solid piece of wood Mike carved a stake, wrote his name on it . . . walked to the middle of the lot, and bending down, drove the stake into the ground—

Now he owned a good-size lot!.

He and Roberto could build a shed to live in. Come Spring he'd start building Mimi's house.

V

Working hard, long hours Mike found he was blowing red dust from planks every time he swung the hammer, but as a carpenter for the Mining Company he was pocketing a good twenty–five cents an hour. Every ten–hour day put two dollars and fifty cents in his pocket. And with Joe Peteli bringing work his way he began building again. First a livery barn, then a store using cement blocks.

June 1904 he was hired to teach woodworking in a new manual training school in Virginia. So he had to go the ten miles to that town two nights a week, and looking around, he bought a brown, two-door coup he would still be driving fifteen years later, *now all I must do is learn to drive . . .*

But he was hungry for Mimi and his children.

Mike also knew that coming to America with Roberto had made all the difference. Now he and Roberto had only to bring Mimi, the children, and Rosa to America. Except for food, and the money sent to Mimi Mike had saved for a two-story wood house . . .

. . . And a backyard privy, *he knew would horrify Mimi.* But Mountain Iron had no water!

June 1904 Mike wrote Mimi:
> *It's the best I can do . . . We will be together, we will take in boarders, you will have to cook. Roberto and Rosa will live with us.   I long for you. — your Mike.*

Mike shouted to wake up Roberto from working late:

"Roberto! We build the house!"

The sun was good, the ground firm, no dust in the wind, and he was up early, stretching, flexing muscles, Roberto joining in even before Mike's whistling started. And thinking of *his little Mimi . . .* Mike was soon singing Italian arias with miners stopping—first to stare—then coming by to listen...

August 1904 Mike had good news for Mimi:

> *My little Mimi, I am building us a house. Minnesota here has much work. It is a different life Mimi, but with much promise. Winter is cold. You must all have warm clothes. Cold on ship too. September when Roberto comes for Rosa —so will I. You must be ready to sail.*
>
> *My little Mimi, I long for you. — your Mike.*

And Mimi wrote quickly: *My Mike . . . Come!*

Two more children were born to Mimi and Mike in America, daughter Lollie who died at eighteen, and their son, Arnold. When many years had passed, on another sunny November day Olympia Catarina 'Mimi' and Massimo Michael celebrated their Fiftieth Wedding Anniversary.

· · · · ·

"I am a good builder, and America must need builders—" Massimo 'Mike' Lenci had told his 'little Mimi.' With his grown son John, he built municipal buildings across Minnesota, the Dakotas, Iowa, Wisconsin.

While Roberto and Rosa followed the scent of grapes to Napa, California, where Roberto, at last, founded his Winery.

WHAT LOVE IS THIS

What love is this to steal my heart!
Carry me far from comfort and home,
Far across an unknown sea,
What love that rages hot in me,
Tears me so asunder—
for
The ocean rolls and heaves and dares,
As to my breasts I clasp my own,
And feel the sea–wind in my hair.
Oh I come Love, I've come at last,
Smile on me once more—
for
I come my love, I come at last,
Oh meet me on that shore.

PINK PETALS FOR MIMI

I brought her one day,
A pretty pink rose,
The sweetest rose from our garden,
And she smiled at me,
Then held me close,
To wipe away a childhood tear,
And teach me many things.

A pretty pink rose,
In a kitchen glass,
Set proudly on Mimi's table,
And while she slept,
The petals fell, from,
Where my love had placed them.

Long gone is she now,
With rosebud cheeks,
Pink petals soft my memory,
For she taught me there,
Beside her chair,
Of love and being a lady.

Love, Laughter and Tears . . .

WOODLAND GODDESS
Ely Lake, Minnesota.

WOODLAND GODDESS

With a pattering of raindrops,
On a breath of wind,
The mind reflects, and words compel,
On fluted leaves, and paper birch,
Between a cabin, and the bay.
Where whispering leaves dip and shimmer,
Seductively caress smooth velvet trunks,
Moaning gently: "rain, rain, rain,"
Turning to catch every precious drop.
Paper birch glistening white at sunrise,
Glowing silver beneath the moon,
In velvet elegance, bound by ebony,
Dressed with flowing amber jewels,
As floating upon a deep breath of wind,
Comes the "rasp-rasp" of birch bark curls,
Golden tresses twirling in the breeze.

THE BIRTH OF A POET

She was but twelve,
A blossoming lass,
And the winter winds blew,
At forty below . . . 'til,
The snow piled up,
To the windowsills,.
She was but twelve,
When the spirit bloomed,
And a poet was born,
On a quiet spot,
On a marble stair,
'tween lunch and classes,
You'd find her there.

She was but twelve,
Worn pencil in hand,
Bent to a task,
That flowed from the soul,
And winter winds died,
The cold snows melted,
Before the intensity,
Of warm brown eyes,
For an inner sun shone,
As she sat alone,
Writing her poems,
Day after day,
When the spirit bloomed,
And a poet was born.

ELIZABETH LENCI–DOWNS...

Elizabeth Lenci-Downs was born in Virginia, Minnesota. *LIZZY - A Special Collection*, reflects her heritage and growing up on the Iron Range where from a young age she wrote stories and poetry. At age sixteen she won The State of Minnesota 2nd Prize for her essay promoting the new Quetico, International Peace Forest. Today Lenci is a writer, artist, historian, and retired educator. Honors include membership in The National League of American Pen Women - in Letters; and Arts; being Awarded 1995 YWCA Woman of the year in Fine Arts for Maricopa, County, Arizona, one of ten outstanding women honored for commitment to the empowerment of women and the elimination of racial discrimination; Juried member of the Arizona Artist Guild. Elizabeth and her husband Floyd L. Downs live in Fountain Hills, Arizona. She would like to be contacted at—
email: lenci.downs@cox.net.
Website with Pay Pal: www.LenciStudios.com.